LIVING WITH THE STORY

Bible Studies For Group Participation

Edited by Sheila Mayo

BIBLE SOCIETY

BRITISH AND FOREIGN BIBLE SOCIETY
Stonehill Green, Westlea, Swindon SN5 7DG, England

First published 1994

Every attempt has been made to trace and correctly attribute the sources of the prayers and material for reflection within this book, although by the very nature of prayers this is difficult to do. Bible Society would gratefully receive any corrections for inclusion in future reprints.

A catalogue record for this book is available from the British Library
ISBN 0564 08595 2

Typeset by BFBS Production Services Department, TP section
Printed in Great Britain by Redwood Books
Cover design by Jane Taylor

Bible Societies exist to provide resources for Bible distribution and use. The British and Foreign Bible Society (BFBS) is a member of the United Bible Societies (UBS), an international partnership working in over 180 countries. Their common aim is to reach all people with the Bible, or some part of it, in a language they can understand and at a price they can afford. Parts of the Bible have now been translated into over 2,000 languages. Bible Societies aim to help every church at every point where it uses the Bible. You are invited to share in this work by your prayers and gifts. Bible Society in your country will be very happy to provide details of its activity.

Contents

Word of God
be in our speaking
Silence of God
be in our listening
Unite us in your peace
and divide us with your sword
Cross of Christ
be in our deciding

John V Taylor

Foreword

This book came to be written or rather "lived" during a four-day conference exploring the many different ways of engaging with the Bible. It was sponsored jointly by the British and Foreign Bible Society, the World Council of Churches, and the YMCA.

Many groups in the United Kingdom have traditionally studied the Bible by a fairly conventional process of reading and dicussion. Sometimes this is an illuminating process which leads the members of the group into new understanding and greater fellowship. However, it is a method of Bible study that doesn't suit everyone's personality, cultural background or learning skills. Often, some people learn more naturally through drama and role-play, by practical activities or even playing games. The conference, which formed the basis for this book, enabled all of us to discover that the Bible can come to life in many different ways, particularly when we look at it in unusual ways.

All the participants came from different Christian traditions (and some from none), and a variety of cultural backgrounds. These diverse people lived, worshipped, studied and enjoyed leisure time together; and, as the week progressed, we encountered the Bible coming to life in each other's lives. It was a week in which the great diversity of human experience was encountered and celebrated as we moulded clay, wrote letters, sat in quiet contemplation and acted out the great stories of faith. Through all this, we heard the voice of God speaking through the scriptures, speaking through our activities — and through each other's experience.

The Bible studies offered in this book may be unfamiliar to many groups in local churches. Yet, they do offer a new way of encountering the living word of God, which was fully revealed in human flesh and blood. They will be particularly appropriate for people who learn more naturally through experience rather than in traditional academic ways. Youth leaders may find some of them appropriate for their groups, and all of them could be used effectively on retreats and conferences. Above all, it is hoped that they will help members of local churches to discover new ways of learning and new ways of discovering the "word made flesh" in the midst of their everyday lives.

There were eight workshops led by Chris Peck, John Vincent, Athene Hariades, Brian Robinson, Jeni Parsons, Bill Denning, Paul Bates, and Alison Norris. The participants were Terry Goodhall,

Arthur and Jackie Rowell, Kemi George-Barbarinde, Vic Vivian, Josie Honey, Natasha Henry, Florence Odulate, Lesley Broad, Sue Lewis, Graham Davies, Ethel Levermore, Jonathan Famoriyo, Veronica Tella, John Gibson. Sheila Mayo was the "writer", Ron Ingamells of the YMCA convened the conference, Wille Riekkinen of the WCC was the theological consultant, and Simon Reynolds of BFBS, joined us for part of the week.

Sadly, two people who took part in the conference died while this book was being written. Florence Odulate died of cancer in 1992; and Athene Hariades died in a road accident in 1993. It is to both these people, and to the memory of their vital and living presence, that this book is dedicated.

Introduction

Bible Study as a Learning Process

Wille Riekkinen

Bible study is always a kind of experiment, a learning process. It is a way of finding out how biblical texts speak to us today and of recognizing the message.

Nowadays we cannot expect to convince our partners in dialogue simply by saying: "It is written in the Bible". The message of the Bible must "become flesh" before it can be effective. That is why the meaning of the texts has first to be clarified; after that, we can reflect on their relevance for today. The message itself must prove its own importance and truth; and so it is important to listen to what God is really saying to us and to our neighbours through the biblical texts we are studying.

Some Methods of Study

There are many aspects of approaches we can experiment with when we engage in Bible study. But first of all, we need to reflect on the unique resource "library" which we call "the Bible" or "the Holy Scriptures".

The Bible consists of 66 volumes which gather up oral and written traditions from more than a thousand years. The oldest traditions were transmitted orally from generation to generation, by reciting them with the accompaniment of music and movement. After hundreds of years they were then written down, edited, published and enriched with new writings. This literature was used for very different purposes, e.g. for festivals in temples, synagogues and early Christian churches, for instruction in faith, and for remembrance of God's great deeds. It was also used to defend or to proclaim the faith, for pastoral consolation or correction in a crisis of faith, for counselling those in positions of power, and for giving hope to the hopeless. Accordingly, we find many different literary types and styles. For example, there are liturgies, poems, stories, genealogies, codes of law, proverbs, letters, satires, words of wisdom, meditations, and visions. The methods of communication are equally varied: we can find recitation, writing, symbolism, historical accounts, intellectual reasoning, prophetic deeds. This richness of biblical material is not to be neglected! We should always take account of such a diversity of styles as we seek to root the message of the Bible in today's complex world.

For example, we can look at three different approaches we can consider when embarking on a Bible study experiment: a historical-literary, a theological-meditative and an existential approach.

Historical-Literary Approach

In each biblical passage individual members of the people of God have put down in writing their own witness to what God taught them and their community. In the Bible we can hear the voices of a personal (or national) relationship to God. So our first step in interpretation is to try to find out what the writers were really saying in the situation in which they lived, in the period from about 1000 BC to AD 140. This will help us when we come to examine what God wants to tell us today through these same scriptures.

The historical-literary approach does not necessarily require academic training. It can proceed by asking a few very simple questions:

a. *who* speaks, *when, where* and to *whom*? The answers to these questions will help us to understand the structure and context of the text being studied. To illustrate the text's political, cultural and religious circumstances we need to have knowledge of the Bible, and sources of information about the whole historical context of the ancient Near East. Modern commentaries and other tools for Bible study (concordances, biblical theological word-books and books on archaeology, history and everyday life in biblical times) can give us the necessary background and "feeling" to understand the text.

b. What is the *literary* type of the passage? Is it a report, a parable, an allegory, a prayer, a hymn, a confession, a satire, a dialogue? Is the author of the book using his favourite terms and images? Is he using symbols? These questions are important because we may misunderstand the text, for example by trying to explain a parable as if it were a report, or a satirical story as if it were a historical event.

c. The questions outlined above will help us to formulate the particular message the original author(s) wanted to communicate to the hearers and/or readers of that time. Is there something new in the message? What is the writer's purpose?

The purpose of questions a, b, and c is to separate the details of historical circumstances from the essential message, and to recognize the impact the message would have made in its original situation. When we have done so, we can think how best to communicate the message in our own situation today. We have to find modern cultural symbols and modern methods. Simply to produce devotions is not enough if we want to let the Bible influence the world today. Here's an example from the book of Jonah:

A Historical-Literary Exercise in the Book of Jonah

1. Read it!
2. What is the structure of the whole story? Who are the actors?
3. What places are mentioned? What does it tell us about the times? When was the story written? Who was the writer?
4. What is the literary type of the story? What symbols are used?
5. Try to understand the story, not as a historical report, but as a satire: What kind of religiosity is criticized here? What is said about the "pious" Jonah? What is he saying about himself in the Psalm of Jonah 2.3–10? Is that true? What is said about God? What is the message of the book of Jonah? Is it adequate for our times?

Theological-Meditative Approach

The questions we asked about the historical-literary approach to Bible study lead us on to the next step which is to reflect on the chosen text theologically. We are expecting God to speak to us through the text. In meditation, we shall try to go beyond our literary and historical study and to reach a theological understanding of the text. To do this, the following aspects should be noted:

a. Biblical texts are expressions of faith based on various theological views developed through the ages. It is important to ask which tradition the studied text belongs to, and which early or later applications of faith are reaffirmed, reinterpreted, or perhaps contested in the text. To arrive at an answer, we must turn once again to the historical understanding of the Bible. In Bible study groups, this information can be given by a suitable resource person (usually the leader of the group). He or she can help the group to think about the content of the faith being expressed in the text. What does the passage say about God — human beings — nature?

b. Many biblical texts are actually prayers. Is this true of the present text? Does it have any ritual significance? Can the message of the text be expressed through contemporary parables, symbols, art forms, body language, mime, drama? If so, why not use them?

As we follow these steps we are trying to find out what God wants to teach us through the experiment of Bible study. If we are to succeed, we should recognize the importance of sharing our findings and learning from each other.

Existential Approach

In our theological-meditative approach we took a step towards the existential approach, which means that we try to apply the message to ourselves in the concrete realities of contemporary society. We discover how we are challenged to respond, and what our responsibilities are. Our context may be totally different from the original life situation of the examined passage. Of course it may be that the text has an immediate relevance to us, and no specific Bible study is necessary; we simply agree with the message of the text. But sometimes it does not "speak" to us. Or sometimes we may remember other texts in the Bible, which may say the opposite (e.g. Romans 13.1–7 compared with Revelation 13 and Acts 5.29). Then we have to find a new direction through self-examination and the encounter of the text with our present life situation. This involves recognizing the challenges, promises, consolation, demands, fear, and sin, that the text conveys to us. But this is no more than a halfway stage; we have to go on to examine what kind of repentance is needed in our life today. Who needs it, why and how? To answer these questions, it is good to learn to read the texts of the Bible through the eyes of the oppressed — and oppressors. We can then understand the different possible interpretations and learn to ask the will of God for us today.

An Exercise on John 4.5–27

1. Read the text responsively.
2. How was the relationship between Samaritans and Jews? Why?
3. How did Jesus approach people?
4. How did the Samaritan woman understand him? Were there misunderstandings?
5. What was the role and message of Jesus?

6. What is the role of the Samaritan woman in the whole story?
7. What is the message for us?

An existential approach alone is always a risk, because we have no control over how our message will be heard. Therefore in every Bible study experiment we must try to take account of all *three* approaches just outlined. Knowledge, spiritual understanding, experience, and feelings belong together. Then comes the important sharing of our findings and learning together.

Techniques for Understanding

The leader of the Bible study group should realize that many participants often only have the vaguest picture of a passage after a first reading. One of the most important steps, even goals, of a Bible study is to ensure that the text is clearly understood. One reading is seldom enough; we need to use our imagination to make the journey through space and time to enable us to "participate" in the "event" described in the text. In Bible study groups we sometimes need to use the same kind of identification techniques that we employ when we read novels and watch films. That is, we must try to feel ourselves to be actually part of the scene being portrayed. This effort can still be intensified through, for example, role-plays, drama, movement, mime, etc. These can form part of the Bible readings as well as of the meditation. Of course this is not suitable for every biblical text, but it is excellent for dialogues and for some of the more dramatic passages of scripture.

An Exercise on Luke 5.17–26

A paralysed man is brought on a bed to Jesus to be healed. The key point is not the method of healing but the new attitude that is demonstrated. The sick man was oppressed by the concept that illness is a terrible punishment sent by God. In this situation Jesus becomes the intermediary between God and the sick man's opponents. Jesus was a subversive in that he showed God to be on the side of the sick. To affirm that his authority came from God, Jesus declared forgiveness of sins to the victim.

But the view-point of the paralysed man (or of Jesus) is not the only one to be considered if we want to make the story real for the members of our group. In a "many roles approach" the text should also be seen through the eyes of the bearers, the Pharisees, and the (uncritical) disciples — then and nowadays! It is good to give these roles to various members of the group. After reading the text, the participants will need some time to reflect on "their" role in the story, so that they can express their feelings, fears, hopes, and motives in small groups or in a general discussion. This process helps to make the text familiar, and the role-play helps us to understand the whole context of the point being made by the biblical author.

This kind of approach helps us to adapt historical facts and exegetical knowledge (historical approach), to use spiritual reflection (meditative approach) and to participate existentially in biblical events and stories. We will be more able to analyse the situation, understand the behaviour of the people involved, and react to the message. The role-players themselves find it an effective experience which makes the story a lasting influence on their lives and thought.

Another useful role-play technique is based on the principles of modern psycho-drama, and is called "living statues". Biblical stories are illustrated and meditated on with the help of imaginary scenes created by a "sculptor" who is a member of the Bible study group. He or she positions volunteer members of the group in the arrangement described in the biblical story. Through these "slides" (3 – 4 "minutes" of the story) the biblical passage can be made real, and the interplay of characters in the story can be underlined. Historical information about the text is needed, and at the same time the "feelings" of the persons involved (in the Bible as well as in the group) can be analysed. Paul's short letter to Philemon can be used to exemplify this approach, proceeding as follows:

1. The historical situation must be explained.

   a. persons: Philemon, a powerful member of the congregation in Colossa. Onesimus, his runaway slave — now coming back as a believer, thanks to Paul, Timothy, and Epaphras.

b. the normal fate of runaway slaves
c. the risk of return
d. Paul's role

2. Action: volunteers take on their roles. One member of the group has to act as "sculptor". He or she creates three scenes by placing the role players in suitable positions. The scenes could be
a. Onesimus escapes from Philemon
b. Paul explains the gospel to Onesimus
c. Onesimus gives Paul's letter to Philemon, who reads it.

After each scene the group leader asks the group to look at the statues and reflect on the message. In the third scene the letter to Philemon is read aloud. Before releasing the last statue, the leader could ask what may have happened to Onesimus — the Bible does not tell us. (We only know that Bishop Ignatius sends greetings to a Bishop Onesimus in Ephesus in the early second century!) Then there are discussions by:
a. small groups
b. the whole group together.

It is amazing how many new observations people can make about this short, too often neglected letter.

These kinds of technical approaches help us to understand biblical texts as coherent passages, and to experience motives, forces and feelings behind them. By acting out these feelings in our Bible study group we can make sure that the texts are understood more deeply than if we use only our intellects to interpret the message of the Bible. All these steps should enable us:
a. to grasp the essential content of each text
b. to translate this message into contemporary life.

The message can be communicated by using whatever modern channels of information the group finds appropriate. One possibility is called "transposition" which means to use "sociodrama". A topic is chosen from the Bible, and the group then acts out the Bible's liberating message in a meaningful contemporary way. The same kind of underlying forces and feelings should be involved as are found in the original text. Most stories and parables of the Bible are suitable to be used in this kind of experiment.

An Exercise on Luke 15.11–32

1. The younger brother. What is positive in his behaviour? What is negative? Who are contemporary "lost people"?
2. The elder brother. What is negative in his behaviour? What is positive? Can you think of any analogies?
3. The role of the father? Analogies?
4. The role of the first listeners, the Pharisees. What would their possible reaction be?
5. The message of the parable — to the Pharisees!?
6. Make a modern version (sociodrama) of the parable, but keep the same message.

There is much good, practical advice given by Hans-Ruedi Weber in his brochure *Experiments with Bible Study* (Biblical Studies, WCC, Geneva 1972, pp. 20ff), from which the following notes are taken:

"Sometimes it is impossible to work in small groups, either because the number of participants is too large; because not enough Bible study enablers and resource persons are available; because the time is too short for breaking up into groups, or because the localities for small group work are not at disposal. In this case it is not necessary to fall back on the traditional biblical teaching through monologues which are so seldom true Bible studies. Even with a group of a hundred or a thousand persons a Bible study enabler can let every member actively participate in the study by using the following *alternative to small group work*:

- After a short introductory period of straightforward teaching about the background of the text to be studied, the enabler stops his exposition with a challenging question concerning the text.
- During a short period of silence all members study the text with a view to answering the question asked. Such periods of silence and individual study are important not only in large plenaries but also in small study groups because not everyone's mind works at the same speed. Slow thinkers are often very deep thinkers!
- This two or three minutes' period of silent individual study should be followed by a period of five to ten

minutes for exchanging the discoveries made by each participant with his or her neighbour. With almost every seating arrangement it is possible for two or three persons to talk together without having to shift their chairs and tables, and without having to go into a time-consuming dividing up into different groups.

- After this, a short period of general discussion between the whole group and the Bible study resource person can follow. When the assembly is too large or the acoustics of the hall are too bad, the assembly can be represented by a panel of about three persons who sit together with the enablers on the platform and have access to a microphone. If the panel members are well chosen and represent the various types of participants, very soon the participants will identify with 'their' spokesman on the panel and in this way indirectly participate in the discussion. (These panel discussions must of course remain spontaneous and *not* be rehearsed beforehand. It does not matter if the Bible study enabler or resource person will sometimes have no answer to questions asked or if the panel discussion runs less smoothly than a well rehearsed TV-show).
- The same process of straightforward teaching, silent individual study, exchange with neighbours and general or panel discussion can be repeated twice or three times without too much fatigue of the participants, because they are really involved in the process of study."

The above described method can also often fruitfully be used for small Bible study groups. Especially the exchange with neighbours before the general discussion is important. This allows the timid and less eloquent participants to formulate first their questions or discoveries in a private discussion before bringing their contribution to the whole of the group (which otherwise they might never dare do). It also gives a chance to "let off steam" to those persons who always must speak, whether they have something to contribute to the subject under discussion or not. Having had the opportunity to talk they are thus enabled to listen. It is a general experience that both small group discussions and large plenary discussions are much better after such a process of private discussions with one's neighbours.

Prelude to Chapters One and Two

Tell me, what is this Gospel of God?

Wille Riekkinen

Any attempt to reflect upon the Bible as a basis for witnessing to the Gospel of God in today's world must start with global perspectives. Nowhere seems very far anymore. The transistor radio and television bring events from the most distant places right into our homes and offices at the very moment things are happening. Journeys to distant places, which would have taken weeks or months only some years ago, can now be completed in hours in jumbo jets. We are also discovering that being close together doesn't make it easier to live in harmony with each other. It makes us more aware of our differences: different background, different cultures, but maybe living in the same place. And sadly, this increases the opportunities for serious conflicts and mutual disruption. Yet, because we are all together in one global village, from which we cannot escape even if we wanted to, we must find ways of settling our differences, justly, before it is too late.

In every age, there have been followers of Jesus Christ who understood that being the body of Christ in the world required them to live in obedience to Christ's will, to create a single new humanity in himself. But many Christians have misunderstood their calling. The record of their behaviour towards other Christians, as well as towards their neighbours of other faiths, is full of ugly incidents. Christians have practised cultural, political, economic, and religious imperialism, even in the name of Christ, and we have to confess it. It is not a story of which we can be proud.

Now that we know so well how to destroy all life on our planet earth in seeking our selfish goals there is a new urgency to find ways of living in harmony with each other, and to show respect for our planet home. But fear alone is poor motivation for seeking life together in one world. Christians are called to find their motivation and their hope in God's promise to make "all things new". So human experience teaches us that the path to new life together is rough and dangerous; but hope in God's promise sustains us. Inspired by this hope, Christians, in recent years, in different places, have been struggling to find ways of living together and following fundamental convictions about life which I would like to share with you.

Firstly, Christians can no longer confess that their disunity is a sin and still go on sinning together day by day, since the church is called to be a sign in the world of what God intends for the world.

Secondly, all people share a common humanity, whatever their race, culture or religion, politics or economics, sex or age. And since no one knows the whole of life's story we need each other's wisdom to piece the story together.

Thirdly, there is a direct relationship between the economic and political weakness of many, and the economic and political power of the few. Therefore, we need new ways of relating to each other that will enable us to deal with the root causes of human injustice throughout the world.

Fourthly, the resources of our planet home are not without limits, but they are adequate for our needs. Therefore, we must be good stewards of all nature's gifts and this means putting firm limits to human greed. Can we do that? If we don't try through Bible studies, who will try?

When people of diverse backgrounds engage in a search for ways of facing any of these questions together in humility and openness to God's guidance, they are involved in *ecumenical* learning. Ecumenical learning is what happens when diverse persons, who are rooted in their own faith traditions and complex experiences of culture, gender, nationality, race, and class, become open and responsive to the richness of perspectives in the struggles of others, together seeking to know God and to be faithful to God's intention in the world.

When participating in ecumenical learning the Bible has an important role to play. The biblical message puts the faith of the people of God in a world-wide context. Possibilities of a new life revealed by God's promises are to become a blessing for all generations of the earth. The Old Testament describes the story of the people of Israel in a way leading our eyes to see all of creation and a life of salvation for all people. The New Testament witness to Christ embraces the unity of all Christians as well as the future of the whole inhabited earth and the entire cosmos. The faith of Christianity has from the very beginning been geared in an all-encompassing sense to our one world, because this word *oikumene* meant originally the whole inhabited earth, and then the Church of Jesus Christ in its universality and unity. Nowadays, it is often interpreted as what we have in common in co-operation with Protestant, Orthodox, or Catholic churches and of course it is not inappropriate to interpret *oikumene* in this way as a co-operation among Christians. Yet in doing so, we have to keep in mind that in fact we only deal with some aspects of the real meaning of the word, because the Gospel of God is meant for everybody, not only for Christians.

Ecumenical learning means biblical learning in two aspects. If Christians from different churches and from different cultures, life-styles and life situations share with each other their understanding of biblical texts and spiritual experiences, the fullness and power of Old and New Testament texts can be better perceived. Ecumenical learning therefore means learning to understand the Bible in more depth *through* others and together with them. It means at the same time a discovery of questions and perspectives in biblical assertions, which are essential for the understanding of the *oikumene*. Ecumenical learning leads us to the Bible and proceeds from the Bible.

When participating in it, we have to keep in mind that Bible study is always a kind of experiment, a learning process. It is a way of finding out how biblical texts speak to us today and recognizing the symbols that carry the message. In ecumenical learning we can do this best in communicating with our fellow believers and also if possible with people of other faiths and even of no faith.

Nowadays, we cannot expect to convince our partners in dialogue simply by saying "It is written in the Bible". The message of the Bible must become "flesh" before it can become effective. Sometime ago, I met a Hindu at an airport somewhere and I was reading the Bible. He asked, "What is it you are reading here?" I answered, "This is the Holy Bible", and then I said: "This is the word of God" and so on, and "It is important". He gave me a big photograph of his home. There were many, many books, the whole series of Veda literature and he said, "Here is the word of God. What do you mean by saying that only one book was the Word of God?" And so, if for any reason we somehow have to explain why the Bible is the Word of God for us, what should we say? We deal with this question later when asking what is meant by saying that one book, the Bible, is the Word of God?

When doing Bible study, when having a dialogue with somebody, we have to pay attention to the language we are using, the religious language. If I am speaking to my daughters about Jesus, and if I started to explain saying "Yes, the first thing you have to remember about Jesus is that he is a High Priest according to the order of Melchizedek", what would happen? They take their bikes and walkmans and disappear, and I have lost my opportunity. This means that we have to find a new language today, even in our Bible studies, to speak about the functions of Jesus, of believing in Jesus, so that we can say what we really mean. It's not enough to say "It is written in the Bible". The message of the Bible must become "flesh" before it can be effective. That is why the meaning of the text has first to be clarified, and there we need common study and common experience and knowledge. After that, we can reflect on its relevance for today and we have to interpret this text anew, otherwise we could be replaced by tape recorders. The message of the Bible itself must prove its own importance and truth. Therefore it is important to really listen to what God is saying to us and to our neighbours in the biblical texts we are studying.

Chapter One

The House of Simon

(Luke 7.36–50)

Chris Peck

This story was shared with us by Chris Peck, Director of Development for Mission in the Anglican Diocese of Liverpool. In our assessments at the end of the session, the crucial areas of sexuality and power were often commented on. Our present thinking and practice as men and women in the church is a mass of contradictions, largely unresolved, because we do not face other options than those to which we are accustomed. We need to be liberated from a masculine and academic theology, and respond to thinking like that of Jesus, open, total, and universal.

Introduction

This is a study in which we will use our imagination to identify with the experience of the characters in a Gospel story, and see how that helps us to enter into the meaning of the story for today. The leader's role is to *facilitate*, not participate.

Exploring Our Experience

(This should take about 1 hour.)

This Bible study will touch upon relationships. In order that participants will be able to engage with each other, they will need to have some level of communication with each other. Try this "ice-breaker":

First introduce yourself to one another, and work in pairs for five minutes. Then work in fours for 10 minutes, asking these questions:

- What would you like to know about someone in order to share with them in a Bible study about relationships?
- Share your favourite Bible story from memory — part of the "Bible" we carry around inside us.

Then, come back together as one group, and say you're going to look at the story of the woman with the jar of precious ointment. Ask people to work in pairs *without using their Bibles* on the following questions:

- What associations and feelings do we have with this story?
- Does it ring bells for any of us?
- How do you recall the story? Where did it happen and when? Who was involved? What happened? What was the point of the story?

Then come back together as one group. Compile the "memories" on a large sheet of paper. When this is done, point out that there are four versions of the story, placed in different positions and times in the Gospels, and all making a different point (Matthew 26.6–13; Mark 14.3–9; Luke 7.36–50; John 12.1– 8). We are going to explore Luke's account.

As one group:

- Read the story, identify yourself with one of the various characters: Simon, guests, Jesus, woman. Then divide up into four groups representing Simon, guests, Jesus and the woman.

In these groups ask:

- What is your situation at the beginning of the story? What happens to you during it? How do you feel at each point?
- What is your situation at the end?

Then, look more closely at the content of the story; and, still identifying yourself with one of the characters, ask the following questions:

Simon:

- Why do you invite Jesus?
- How do the other guests feel?

Jesus:

- What is going on for you at this point?

Woman:

- As you approach what are you feeling?
- As you enter, what happens?

How do others react to this interruption:
Guests?
Simon?
Jesus?

Then, as the situation in the story changes, and Simon complains to Jesus and hears Jesus' reply, ask what's going on for these characters:
Guests?
Woman?

When Jesus turns to the woman what's going on there?

Finally, come out of your "rôle", and reflect upon your experience as one of these characters.

Studying the Context

(This should take about 1 hour.)

Firstly, begin by considering Luke as the unseen character, and ask the following questions:

- What do we know about Luke and his gospel?
- What comes before this story in his gospel? (for example, two healings: Centurion's servant and the Widow of Nain's son; then John's question to Jesus, and Jesus' answer in verse 22:
  "the blind can see,
  the lame can walk,
  those who suffer from dreaded skin-diseases are made clean,
  the deaf can hear,
  the dead are raised to life,
  and the Good News is preached to the poor.
  How happy are those who have no doubts about me!")

Listen to the story again, and ask:

- What are the issues addressing us today?
- What actions are we called upon to take in the light of the story?

Evaluation

After the two-hour session, we met to evaluate the experience of studying this passage. Here are some of the questions raised to aid evaluation.

- What was good?
- How did you feel while taking part in the study?
- What was bad?
- What new learning insights did you gain?
- Did it help personally?
- How could we improve it?

Eternal God,
as you created
humankind
in your own image —
women and men,
male and female,
renew us
in that image.
Amen.

Sheila Mayo

Chapter Two

The Cost of Discipleship

(The Gospel Of Mark)

John Vincent

This session was led by John Vincent, a Methodist Minister from Sheffield, who is well known as the Director of the Urban Theology Unit, and the founder of the Ashram Community which exists for those who have joined together to support each other in discipleship. This leads into practical action. As John commented, "we search for appropriate ways to change our lifestyle, to take account of a divided world, and a divided Britain; we try to make our life decisions about jobs, vocation, use of money, place to live and work, and practise action, all in relation to the Gospel".

Introduction: the Method

This session is based on "Snaps", a game in which people are asked to use their imagination to see connections between the situation in the gospel and our own situation. Within this "game", the following elements need to be used:

1. *Snaps* — when we see a "snap" between a story in our own life or world, and a story in the gospel.

2. *Studies* — when the text is thought about objectively, but using methods of identification with characters in the stories, asking questions like "What is happening to us as characters in this story?" "Why, as Mark, have we put this story in at this point?" In addition, more traditional ways of understanding the text are used — we study the text in the context of its social, cultural, historical and theological background.

3. *Spin offs* — in which the group moves on to implications for decisions in their own context. What might we do today which would be "like" this biblical story? What might we do today that could use this biblical story as "justification" or explanation?

Finding "Snaps"

Start with an example:

"a group of old people are in the temple waiting for the coming of the Lord. . ."

Then try some more:

virgin birth. . .
walking on the water. . .
feeding of the five thousand. . .
the prodigal son. . .
the call of the first disciples. . .

Several members of the group responded with stories:

So. . . already I am in the story —
I am a parent, waiting. . .
I am the small boy with loaves and fish. . .
I am the younger brother. . .
I am the elder brother. . .
I am the father. . .
I am sitting around waiting for a call. . .

Then, with this "snap", move on to the next stages.

Studies

What actually happened in the gospel story?
What did it really feel like for the person I "snap" with?
What resulted for them?

Spin Offs

What might it lead me to?
What from the results in the story do I have to learn?

Finding "Patterns"

The method of snaps-studies-spin offs can be developed further in two ways:

1. Sequences: we can take a series of gospel stories and happenings and ask, (or could do) "how does the way one thing comes after another suggest or illustrate the way things happen one after another in my life or world?"

2. Patterns: we can take several incidents that belong to the same longer story and ask, "how does a pattern of one story

later on in the gospel develop and take further something begun in an earlier story?"

Take *Discipleship to Jesus* in Mark's Gospel. There are at least five "*stages*" which form a "pattern" of discipleship:

1.	Mark 1.17–18; 2.23	"Come with me"	Following
2.	Mark 4.11	"You have been given the secret of the Kingdom of God"	Intimacy
3.	Mark 6.8	"Don't take anything with you. . ."	Mission
4.	Mark 8.34–35	"Cross bearing"	Pain/joy
5.	Mark 10.29–31	"Losses and gains in the new community"	One hundred-fold

The Pattern of Discipleship

"Play" this sequence of snaps-studies-spin offs. (We have provided some of the responses that came out of our group study.)

Snap	**Study**	**Spin Off**	**Participant's Reactions**
1. Following Mark 1.17–18, Mark 2.23	Come follow me; first following	Starting out	Being brought into the activity of Jesus; to get behind him; be named by his name; be associated with his movement; be a worker in his task force actually achieving things (fisher of people)
2. Intimacy Mark 4.11	Initiation into secrets	Heightened awareness	Being declared by Jesus to be on his side; to be part of his movement; party to his action; party to his secrets; included in his kingdom (even though he does not actually explain anything to us!)
3. Mission Mark 6.7	Sending out on mission, two by two to exercise with rule	Practice working in the mission	Being out together with immense expectations, on an impossible task, yet which is all joy, under a shared discipline, totally dependent on others, whose response to the message is response to the Kingdom
4. Cross-bearing Mark 8.34	Further following as cross-bearing, self-denial	Pain, losses	Being near to death? or drowning, as in "burn out"? Being taken deeper down, when I've already 1. given up all to follow 2. been brought into the secrets 3. been a co-worker with him but now to be told I have to take his/my cross on top of it all
5. Receiving back Mark 10.29–31	Losses and gains	Joy— the hundred-fold return	Being prepared that I will make my delights (or compensations!) out of exactly the same thing/people as I suffered my losses in (the same items in both lists!) Being happy that the whole thing of new brothers and sisters is actually OK; that the struggle is a struggle made possible by fellow-strugglers; that the Body of Christ ever constitutes itself again

Note: This method was developed in J D Davies and J J Vincent, *Mark at Work* (Bible Reading Fellowship, 1986) revised edition forthcoming. See also J Davies, *World on Loan* (Bible Society, 1993), J J Vincent, *Mark's Gospel in the Inner City* (Urban Theology Unit, 1993), J J Vincent, "Inner City Bible" in Dan Cohn–Sherbok (ed.), *Using the Bible Today* (Bellew Publishing, 1991).

Give me,
O Lord my God,
an understanding that
knows you,
wisdom in finding you,
a way of life that is
pleasing to you,
perseverance
that faithfully waits for
you,
and confidence that I may meet
you
at the end

Thomas Aquinas

Interlude

Sheila Mayo

"No one can step more than once into the same river because the water flowing into it is not the same water that flowed there yesterday. It is a different river."

In our imaginations we have tried to be present with Simon in his house. He has done his best to provide a welcome for Jesus but a guarded one. No washing of the feet, no kiss, no anointing, and then the woman came and brought disturbance and embarrassment. And Jesus, accepting her and affirming her, mildly rebukes the host, saying, "Simon, you gave me no water but she has washed my feet with her tears and dried them with the hairs of her head." This strange prophet was forever turning things upside-down!

And in another group we have experienced in part the cost of discipleship, women and men "on the road" tired, quarrelsome, suspicious, alternately astonished and dismayed by this mysterious rabbi who called them to live and die with him.

In the early morning some of us went for a walk by the river on the east side of Dunford House near the dining room where we ate together, below the chapel and the table tennis room, deep in the woods. The sounds of silence: birds; a breeze and a blue cloudy sky. And the water singing away quietly in the deep chine — as John Vincent had said "God streams out of all of it". Not only from the beautiful countryside surrounding Dunford but from the urban areas from which many of us came. It was good to be reminded of Richard Cobden who was born and died in the house. He was a colleague of Wilberforce in the abolition of the slave trade, and often carved his bread at meal times with these words:

> *Do you wish the food of your children to be taxed, and the food of your pigs to be free?*

In his political work, and his life as a Christian, Richard Cobden challenged the entrenched assumptions of his age. Through our Bible study, we are opening ourselves to the constant challenge of the Gospel.

In our walk we explored what *was* the "good news" for us, women and men, in the world-wide church. We realized that this gospel is free, new every morning, that it cannot be stored, but only be experienced and given away. In our prayers we remembered the outsider, the secret believer.

Material for Prayer and Reflection

"Is it possible that our age is past, and the gospel entrusted to another people, perhaps to be preached with quite other words and deeds?"

"Here I meet people as they are, far from the masquerade of the Christian world. . .small groups, with small aims, small wages, and small sins. . .people we feel homeless in both senses. . .real people. I can only say that to me it seems that people stand in God's grace rather than his anger, and that it is much more the Christian world which stands his anger rather than his grace."

Mary Bosanquet, *The Life & Death of Dietrich Bonhoeffer*

When I first came to religion I wanted to know more about God because I was frightened of knowing too much about myself. Lots of people use piety to evade or avoid. But as the kingdom of heaven is within you, you can't know one without knowing the other, and if you try it produces some strange and nasty results such as fanaticism, holy wars, and persecution. The doubts we suppress inside ourselves become the "heretics" we suppress in the world outside.

I've ruminated a lot about my own life, partly because I am self-absorbed like most pious people and partly because I want to locate the divinity within me and not just another hang up.

It is tempting to leave out the sex bit, and the silly bit, but the result would be too sanitary and false. I rely on religion to help me not to be sensitively selective. I may pretend I am only trying to protect religion, the truth is I am ony protecting me.

Christ Jesus,
whose glory was poured like perfume,
and who chose for our sake
to take the form of a slave:
may we also pour out our love
with holy extravagance,
that our lives may be fragrant with you,

Amen.

Janet Morley, *All Desires Known*, SPCK, 1992

Prelude to Chapters Three and Four

A new, fresh way to be and act

Wille Riekkinen

This meditation was given during an act of worship, at which the reading was Mark 1.14 –15.

In the Prelude to chapters 1 and 2, I reflected upon the gospel of God which Jesus preached and asked, What does it mean? What was its content? What was at that time the transforming, liberating, saving gospel? This gospel of God has a very rich background. It is not only "resurrection" and "Easter"— which belong to the gospel of Jesus. The gospel of God is something else!

In the Old Testament also there are many references to the gospel as "good tidings" from God to his people. From these writings we can see that "the Kingdom of God" no longer denotes *place* or *time* but the action of God wherever and in whomever. Somebody has even proposed that perhaps we should stop talking about "the Kingdom of God" at least in many places in the world; because for so many peoples it brings only bad images to mind.

That is why the phrase has to be re-translated if it is to be correctly understood. The question concerning the Kingdom message of Jesus is therefore a very important one when we try to understand what he meant, and what this can mean for us today. The phrase does not occur in the Old Testament, though there are nine references to God ruling *in* a Kingdom.

The faith of the New Testament rests on two certainties, one that God had come in the past and then died for his people; and secondly the firm hope that God will come anew now and in the future to accomplish his purposes. According to Mark 1.14–15 which was our starting point, Jesus' great news was that this "Kingdom" is now at hand. This Kingdom has to do with the power that permits all space and all time rather than being limited by space and time. The early Church looked upon God's Kingdom as already present during Jesus' ministry, and as a power yet to come.

Mark seems to imply that for his day and his readers the Kingdom was already there. "The Kingdom of God has arrived", he says, and from this the implication is clear. The *kairos* (right time) is fulfilled precisely because the Kingdom has already appeared and the time of salvation is at hand. But now we still need to clarify what we mean by "salvation".

We have seen that there are several aspects of salvation in the Wisdom literature and the history of Israel, from the lifetime of Jesus, from after Easter, and in the life of the early church. But we can look at another passage, Luke 19.1–10 (the story of Zacchaeus). It speaks of salvation in *this* life. There is no reference here to Jesus' death and resurrection. He simply spoke of salvation because it was his job to do so, to bring these people to God; to give birth to belief in God. Somehow I always see ways of salvation in Israel's history both before the death of Jesus as well as after. We are very lucky in having these ways, because we can use all of them. We are not restricted only to Jesus' life, death, and resurrection. We have to remember all mighty deeds of God.

For Zacchaeus salvation meant *relationship to God*, something happened in his heart. It means relationships to others. He was sorry for what he had done wrong and made a change in his way of living. Now that he has a working relationship with God he wanted to act accordingly. Can you think of ways in which you have experienced salvation like that — either in your own life or in the lives of others?

When we talk about salvation we sometimes use dogmatic statements about "resurrection", "doomsday", etc. At the one extreme we have a concept of salvation in the future, so that our present life has only meaning for thereafter. The result is sometimes a total withdrawal from the problems of society. I think this is a misunderstanding of the gospel. At the other extreme, the only salvation which fits this present age is thought to be salvation in terms of economic and political issues, more or less in the hands of human beings. The result here can be a total preoccupation with these issues in terms of social progress with no reference to spiritual values. Again, this shows a misunderstanding of the Bible.

Jesus preached "salvation" as means to have a living relationship with God so that "eternal life" can begin here and now; touching all aspects of our existence, relating not only to our earthly life but to life after death.

For another contrast, we can look at one more text, Matthew 4.23, and discover much about teaching, preaching, healing. Service and teaching, word and action belong together. This requires a holistic concept of salvation, including the whole human being, and cannot be reduced to either of the extremes I have tried to describe.

Exercise
Break up into twos or fours, and consider what kind of practical action for the furtherance of the Kingdom you are going to do and demonstrate today. Then ask, in the light of your discussions, what your personal understanding of salvation is.

Chapter Three

The Myrrh-Bearing Women

(A Contemplative Approach)

Athene Hariades

This session was one in which we heard "news" which was new to most of us: the story of the myrrh-bearing women based on the liturgy of the Eastern Orthodox Church. This was shared with us by Athene Hariades, a young Greek woman who illuminated the text not only by her faith, but by means of slides and music relating to the worship of the Orthodox Church. A post-graduate student at the University of Manchester, she helped us to learn that "Orthodox liturgy is long ... you walk in and out of it ... ". This helped us to enter more fully into an approach to Bible study within a fully liturgical context, which includes reference to icons, to the writings of the early Fathers, and to sacred music.

This method of engaging with the Bible might be done most effectively within a setting for worship, with an icon surrounded by candles as the central focus, and with appropriate music from the Orthodox tradition.

"The Myrrh-Bearing Women" is the name given by the Orthodox Church to those women-disciples, who proved themselves faithful to Christ throughout his ministry and after his death on the cross. On examining the text of the gospels, we find that evangelists differ as to their names and numbers; after looking at a rich variety of spiritual sources, I find that any impression of confusion disappears when I study the gospel account of any one of these women.

For those who are outside the Orthodox tradition, the place and function of the icons in worship may be difficult to understand — just as we Orthodox often find it difficult to come to terms with some aspects of Western worship.

An Orthodox church without its icons is almost unimaginable. The justification for the performance of acts of worship in front of the icons, such as the lighting of candles or burning of incense, is to be found neither in Holy Scripture nor the teachings of the early Fathers, but in historical tradition. In the eighth century the icons were a subject of argument between iconoclasts (the destroyers of icons) led by the Emperor Leo III in 730, as a reaction against what these people believed to be an idolatrous veneration of graven images, and the iconodules (those who were in favour of icons). The latter won the day, and the question was settled once and for all at the Second Council of Nicaea in 787, when the Church was still undivided.

The spiritual and theological significance of the icon was formulated at that Council. The icon is primarily neither a "visual aid" nor a work of art, to be appreciated solely for its aesthetic qualities: first and foremost, it possesses a sacramental character, serving as a channel of divine grace. It is a means of sanctification, a window to transfiguration and a focus for prayer. Thus, though it is important that an icon painter should be artistically gifted and should use that gift to the full, he must also prepare himself spiritually for his work: he often prays as he paints. In his work he should reflect not his own subjective vision, but the mind of the Church. Artistic creativity is not excluded, but is to be exercised within prescribed rules. The icon translates material substance into a spiritual image. Indeed Christ, who is the image or icon of the invisible God, has through his incarnation made possible a representational religious art, which in the form of an icon affirms not only the authenticity of Christ's physical body, but also the spirit-bearing potentialities of things.

The gospel stories are, as Bishop Kallistos Ware says, "a form of verbal icon". In a summary of the principal mysteries of the Christian faith from his work, *The Fount of Wisdom*, St John of Damascus writes:

> *"When he had freed those who were bound from the beginning of time, Christ returned again from among the dead, having opened for us the way to resurrection." For the early icon painters the resurrection was a subject so holy and mysterious that it could not be portrayed. Indeed it was not until the tenth century, in Ottonian Germany that anyone dare to imagine and depict the risen Christ. The mystery of Christ's return from among the dead, of his resurrection, which is beyond comprehension, is normally expressed by the icon of Myrrh-Bearing Women at the sepulchre.*

According to the Gospel of St Matthew, the women witnessed an earthquake and saw an angel descend from heaven and roll back the stone; they noticed the fear of the watch, placed there by the Jewish leaders, but neither they nor even the keepers of the tomb were witnesses of the resurrection itself. The angel removed the stone not in order that the risen Christ might come out, but to show that he was no longer inside. The angel's proclamation, "He is not here for he is risen", was intended to enable those who sought "Jesus who was crucified" to see with their own eyes the place where the Lord lay. This means that the resurrection had already occurred before the angel's descent and before the stone was rolled away. The resurrection was an event inaccessible to any eye and beyond all comprehension. In accordance with the gospel story, the icon represents the burial cave in which are the empty sepulchre with the linen cloth lying upon it. Beside it stands the group of myrrh-bearing women and on the stone sit either one or two angels in white garments indicating to the women where the body of Jesus had lain. The great icon painter Ouspensky explains how the composition of this icon is usually quite straightforward, apart from winged figures of the angels in snow-white garments, which give an impression of austere and calm solemnity.

It is interesting to learn from Ouspensky that later, in the seventeenth century, another composition was combined with the icon just described, namely the appearance of Christ to Mary Magdalene. This addition is apparently related to the appearance in Western images of Christ arising from the grave. In response to the need to see the Risen Christ, icon-painters found a means of representing him in an icon without contradicting the gospel story. These two successive moments are represented simultaneously in one composition. The myrrh-bearers, standing closer to the sepulchre, listen to the words of the angel, while Mary Magdalene looks around and sees the Lord, who stands in the centre of the icon in a landscape of small hills. Moreover, since Mary Magdalene had mistaken him for an ordinary man, the gardener, his glorified state is not indicated in any way and he is depicted in the usual garments he wore before the crucifixion. As we have already said, the Evangelists speak differently of the number of both myrrh-bearers and angels. Therefore, as Ouspensky tells us, the number of the women varies according to which gospel story is the basis of the composition. However, the differences do not constitute a contradiction. Andrew Grabar, in his study of the origins of Christian icongraphy, says that it is most common to see two or three Marys depicted in an icon, as this was the minimum number of witnesses to a burial required by Jewish Law.

Fathers of the Church, such as St Gregory of Nyssa and St Gregory Palamas, consider that the myrrh-bearing women visited the sepulchre several times and that each time, their number was different; thus each

Evangelist describes only one of these visits. St Luke gives no number at all, which explains why in certain icons they may number five or more. However, in the majority of icons their number does not exceed that indicated in the Gospels of St Matthew (two) and St Mark (three). Generally speaking, this icon of Easter while bearing testimony of resurrection, is an exact interpretation of the gospel stories down to the smallest details: "... and the cloth which had been round Jesus' head. It was not lying with the linen wrappings but was rolled up by itself" (John 20.7). Such attention to seemingly insignificant detail only emphasizes the incomprehensible character of the event that had just occurred.

Let us now examine how the gospels are used in church services during the Pascal-tide (from Easter Day to Pentecost) to illustrate the resurrection, particularly those passages bringing in the myrrh-bearers.

April 1991 in the Orthodox Church began with the feast of the glorious Resurrection of Christ and continued with the period of 50 days when the liturgical cycle of the Church emphasizes the life-giving victory of Christ. Traditionally there is no kneeling or prostration during this whole period because we now have in our minds, as we pray, the certainty that Christ has raised us with him to stand in the presence of his father and ours. It is during this period that all gospel readings in services are taken from St John. Beginning at the liturgy of the resurrection on Easter Saturday night right up to Pentecost, we read almost the whole of St John's Gospel in order. One exception to this is on the Sunday of the myrrh-bearing women, the third Sunday of Easter, when their story is read from the Gospel of Mark. It may seem strange that two weeks after we have celebrated Christ's rising from the dead and after we have observed his various resurrection appearances through reading and prayers of the Church, we are now taken back on this Sunday to the morning of the resurrection.

The Church has chosen on the Sundays immediately following Easter to show us how certain of our Lord's disciples responded to his dying. First there is the Sunday of Unbelieving Thomas, then we meet the myrrh-bearing women (and Joseph of Arimathea and Nicodemus) who quietly and secretly did what they could to express their love for the one who, as they believed, had left them. The honour that the Church pays these women disciples is a pointer to the fact that what is offered to God out of love for him should never be trivialized or despised. Something done out of love for God, even when we feel that he has abandoned us, may lead us into a deeper mystery.

When we look at the icon of the myrrh-bearing women — one of the icons of the resurrection — we see the moment when the women's sorrow and hopelessness is turned into joy by the angel who tells them "He is Risen". Among the chants on Easter Night are the words, "The women came with myrrh to anoint Christ, the myrrh of God".

A visit by the women to the tomb of the one whom they loved so much is entirely natural. Indeed in some Orthodox countries the custom of pouring oil and wine over the grave during burial is still practised today, and some women probably brought these offerings. This must explain why so many references to the myrrh-bearers are found in the services of the Church. Especially the weekly Saturday vespers and Sunday matins and during Holy Week and Pascal-tide. Some of the women are named; those unnamed may have included the "woman that was a sinner", (Luke 7.37), who anointed Christ in the house of Simon and whom we commemorate on Holy Wednesday. On that evening the sacrament of the anointing of the sick is celebrated in Orthodox churches and all are anointed whether physically ill or not; for there is no clear distinction between bodily and spiritual sickness, and this sacrament confers not bodily healing, but also, forgiveness of sins. Returning to the group of women devotees of Christ, the songs of the Church lay a constant emphasis on the sorrow and tears of the myrrh-bearers. In order to understand the true nature of the grief and tears of these women, we need to examine ourselves and then we discover how sorrow is transmuted to joy in the light of Christ's resurrection. By realizing our own sinfulness we are in turn made aware of the significance of the cross and the burial of Christ. For, after all, there is a relation between the depth of our sin and the depth of love and mercy of God.

Our response to this discovery of darkness and sinfulness within us is surely one of sorrow. Yet this grief is a necessary step on the path to our healing and joy. After all even the Gospel message, the message of joy, is intended for those who are filled with sadness and sorrow by the human condition. According to Matthew 5.4 Christ cries out "Blessed are they that mourn". So we must experience mourning and sadness if we are to understand ourselves fully. One of the most revered of early Orthodox saints, Isaac of Syria, describes in a homily how we may enter into this grief:

Let us entreat the Lord with unrelenting mind to grant us mourning. For with its help we shall enter in to purity. . .

Blessed are the pure in heart, for there is no time they do not see the sweetness of tears, and in this sweetness they see the Lord.

Returning to the grief of the myrrh-bearing women, we should remember that they, like ourselves, were once gripped by sickness of soul. As the gospel tells us, before they became followers of Christ and served him, some of these women were purged of evil spirits and infirmities, such as Mary Magdalene (Luke 8.2). Their healing in the light of Christ brought them the true gift of grief which purged them of their sins and they have become blessed with the joy of the resurrection. In terms of women's roles and perspectives, the myrrh-bearing women are often taken as our model: it was they who served, who provided for Christ and his disciples, and who unlike most of the male devotees of Christ, continued their ministry and devotion to the very end. It was these women, who came to the tomb in one last act of loving-kindness and thus became the heralds of the resurrection.

If we contemplate the icon of words in the Orthodox hymns for the Paschal-tide, we may begin to see that this group of women, along with the Blessed Virgin Mary, represent an icon of the sorrow of all women. In his crucifixion Christ took upon himself this sorrow, which began with Eve, and thus purged it of all self-pity and sickness. It is now a sorrow carrying the sweetness that St Isaac describes and which is symbolized by the sweet smelling ointments that these women bear.

Since there is only one reference in the Paschal-tide narrative to the presence of the Blessed Virgin Mary (John 19.25–28), it is for the individual icon-painter to decide whether or not to show her. However, the hymns of the Orthodox Church at this season are full of references to her experience of the passion of Christ. The Vespers of Good Friday are dominated by the Lamentations of the Virgin:

Alone among women, without pain I bore my child,
But now at thy passion I suffer unbearable pain.

Later the Blessed Virgin calls upon the myrrh-bearing women to join her; we can imagine her surrounded by them for support. At the moment when we recall that Christ's resurrection draws near, the choir sing a hymn to the Blessed Virgin Mary, which begins:

O Virgin, Who hast borne the Giver of Life,
Thou hast delivered Adam from sin
And to Eve hast brought joy in place of sorrow.

Singing the Evlogitaria (see p. 37), we acknowledge not the triumph over sorrow, but the triumph of sorrow. Because we have entered into the experience of Christ's passion during Lent, we can identify with the myrrh-bearing women as their sorrow is turned to joy.

Through contemplating these women in the icons, the gospel-narratives and the Paschal-tide music, we, who did not experience the empty tomb, can begin to understand its significance, but we cannot fully receive the joy of the resurrection with empty hands. For it is not a gift into emptiness, but rather a transformation of a reality that itself years to be transformed. Father Nicholas Behr has beautifully described the phenomenon of the myrrh-bearing women in these words:

> *They went bearing in their hands the sweetness of that sorrow, which enables us to see the resurrection. In this way, too, we may respond with amazement and fear of the great event, like the myrrh-bearing women themselves.*

Finally I should like to share with you the words of a number of non-Orthodox students from King's College, London, who visited Russia at Easter 1991, and who evidently responded to the resurrection in this manner.

> *To travel in Holy Russia during the Easter was especially poignant. As Christ was raised from the dead, we were witnesses to the resurrection of his Church in Russia after 74 years of absolute state suppression. . . In the strength of the little old women who populate the growing churches, we saw the spirit of persistence and devotion that has kept the joy of Christianity ringing in Russia's bleak heart. In the joyful singing of those women we heard again that first realized hope: those early-morning cries at the sight of the empty tomb. It is by their strength that this part of the Christian Church in Russia prepares to face a difficult but, we all believe, glorious future.*

An Orthodox Chant

Evlogitaria (tone 5)

Blessed art Thou, O Lord teach me thy statutes.
The company of angels was amazed beholding Thee, O Saviour, numbered among the dead who hast destroyed the power of death and raised up Adam with thyself setting all men free from hell.

Blessed art Thou, O Lord teach me thy statutes.
"Why mingle ye sweet-smelling ointment with tears of pity O ye women disciples" cried the angel who shone as lightning within the tomb to the myrrh-bearing women. "Behold the tomb and understand: for the Saviour hath risen from the grave."

Blessed art Thou, O Lord, teach me thy statutes.
The myrrh-bearing women hastened early in the morning into thy tomb, lamenting but the angel arose before them, and he said: "the time for lamentation has ceased, weep not, but tell the apostles of the resurrection."

Blessed art Thou, O Lord, teach me thy statutes.
The myrrh-bearing women with their spices came lamenting to thy tomb, O Saviour. But the angel spake unto them, saying: "Why count ye the living among the dead for as God, He hath risen from the tomb."

Glory be to the Father and to the Son and to the Holy Ghost.
Let us worship the Father, together with his Son and the Holy Ghost the Holy Trinity one in essence crying with the seraphim: holy, holy art Thou, O Lord.

Now and for ever and world without end. Amen.

O Virgin who hast borne the giver of life, Thou hast delivered Adam from sin and to Eve Thou hast brought joy in place of sorrow. He who took flesh from Thee, who is both God and man hath restored to the path of life those who had fallen away.

Alleluia, alleluia, alleluia.
Glory be to Thee, O God.

Bible Passages Used during this Meditation
Matthew 20.21–23; 28.1–16
Mark 15.40–41; 16.1–9
Luke 7.37; 8.2
John 11—21, especially 11.2; 19.25–28,38; 20.3–18

Chapter Four

The Seven Letters

Brian Robinson

Brian Robinson presented the Letters to the Seven Churches of Asia. "The Seven Letters" are the answer of the spirit to the fears and perils of Asian Christians towards the end of the first Christian century, and provide a study in which the historical and geographical situation of the participants is most explicit and appropriate. Ephesus the great seaport; Pergamum the granite citadel; Thyatira with its market place and guilds; Laodicea with its streams and conduits and hot springs, and the ever-present gods and goddesses. Does our "Kingdom thinking" give any adequate response to a climate of uneasiness and fear? Are we ready to move from an insular and national theology to one which is global and unrestricted by boundaries?

Outline of the Session

1. Introduction to Apocalypse, Apocalyptic and the Seven Churches.
2. Analysis of the Seven Churches with the aid of the pattern for assessment discovered.
3. Drafting of a letter by each participant in class based on the pattern of assessment found in the Seven Letters.
4. Reading of and responses to the drafted letters by group participants.

Introduction to the Apocalypse, Apocalyptic and the Seven Churches

The Church

a. The book of Revelation receives its titles from the Greek word "*apocalypsis*" (Revelation 1.1), meaning unveiling, revealing, revelation.

b. Apart from perhaps the reading of the letters to the seven churches, Revelation, as a book, is greatly neglected by many Christians. This is due largely to the strange style in which its message has been couched and written.

c. Although the forms of expression communicated are within the idioms of the Hebrew mind, the book appears obscure and remote from our methods of thought and expression.

d. Whether or not the Church Fathers were familiar with the Apocalypse is a matter of varying scholarly opinion. Parallels can be made in Revelation and the *Shepherd of Hermas* (a second-century manuscript written in Greek, from a series of visions) in respect to both textual references (to the tribulation), and the imagery found in the two works (such as the Church as a woman, the enemy as a beast, the apostles as being part of a spiritual building, etc.).

e. While this evidence is not conclusive, there is certainly strong evidence of a wide circulation of the book in the period subsequent to the Apostolic Fathers. With this is also the clear acceptance of the Apocalypse into the Christian canon of Scripture. For example, "the Muratorion Canon shows that no doubts existed over the Apocalypse in the Roman Church towards the end of the second century". Also, it is cited as Scripture in the Letter of the Churches of Vienne and Lyons.

Literary Style

a. The four basic categories of literary genre found in the New Testament are:

(i) Gospel
(ii) Acts
(iii) Epistle
(iv) Apocalypse

b. The book of Revelation falls into the category of apocalypse.

c. An apocalypse is a book containing real or alleged revelations of heavenly secrets or of events that will accompany the end of the world and the inauguration of the kingdom of God.

d. Certain characteristics attend apocalyptic style. These include:

(i) The use of symbolic language — creatures, numbers, astral phenomena, cosmological phenomena, angels.

(ii) The author's use of a pseudonym to give validity to the message of the apocalyptist (since the prophets have ceased).

(iii) Rewritten history — in an attempt to give theological explanation to the present circumstances in form of a prophecy down to their day.

(iv) Pessimism as to the present age; optimism as the age to come.

e. The Apocalypse of John bears some of the above characteristics. In some respects, however, it remains distinct from Jewish apocalypses. John declares his name and assumes he is known. His Apocalypse also shares the optimism of the Gospel rather than the pessimism of apocalyptic thought. Again, the book is prophetic and, instead of ethical passivity, it possesses moral urgency.

The Message

a. Regardless of whether the Revelation was last in order of the New Testament books to be written, it is final in its thought. In it the expectation and consummation of the Church and the ages is portrayed as being fulfilled.

b. Our understanding of the message will be partly influenced by the interpretational approach to the book as a whole.

c. There are four main schools of interpretation:

(i) Preterist — relates only to events of its day

(ii) Historical — a prophecy of the history of the Church

(iii) Idealist — a symbolic picture of the struggle between good and evil

(iv) Futurist — from an extreme viewpoint, this would be seen as part of God's plan for the future of the community; a more moderate view would be to see it as a reflection of the historical situation of the Seven Churches in the light of the prophetic message of the book.

d. In the main, the book addresses prophetically the consummation of the ages, and enunciates abiding principles of a permanent message (faith triumphs over might, the inevitability of judgement, the sovereignty of God through Christ in history). Nevertheless, its immediate and local message to the Churches of Asia cannot be overlooked.

e. Both comfort and caution, set against the backdrop of the consummation of the ages, with a view to sustaining hope despite opposition, from the message of the Apocalypse to the seven churches.

The Seven Churches

a. The Seven Churches were situated on a Roman postal route, beginning with Ephesus and progressing through Smyrna, Pergamum, Thyatira, Sardis, Philadelphia, to Laodicea. From these centres the whole province could be reached.

b. The special circumstances of each of these churches hold forth a particular message to the Church at all times of its history. Some, as we have seen, would hold them as symbolic of set dispensations, which would render their particular message obsolete to our times and thus unable to speak relevantly to our personal lives today.
c. However, not only do we discover a particular word of God to us through the interpretation of the Seven Letters, we also discover a pattern by which Christ analyses each of these congregations.
d. This pattern asks questions of their congregational life in terms of:

(i) Strengths
(ii) Barriers
(iii) Interventions
(iv) Promises
(v) Reservations

e. This study uses Christ's assessment pattern in this study:

(i) to see his analysis of the Seven Churches (see pp. 44–45)
(ii) to give an example of its application in letter form to an existing church today
(iii) to each draft a letter, based on the assessment pattern, to your own congregational situation
(iv) to share our responses with a view to hearing Christ address us in our local settings
(v) to recommend the assessment pattern to our congregations

Using the Assessment Pattern

Having outlined the context and theology of the book of the Apocalypse, members of the group were then asked to consider a contemporary church situation where similar challenges and problems existed, and to write a letter to that church based on the assessment pattern already explored.

Here is an example of the participants' response:

A Message To The Church In England
Unto the angel of the Church in England write: These things says he who is one in the Father and who wishes us to be in him. I know your word that in your devotions and oneness

in Christ you wish to draw your people unto the Father and you have many resources to do so.

Nevertheless I have a few things against you. Some follow not me but the spirit of the ages and think in complexity. These I will allow to go their own way. Others compromise unity by not sharing the unique way I am leading them. Beware of them that do not let my children work for me.

But unto you, study my purposes for this land. Use my spiritual riches given daily and be my witnesses, that they may believe and be one with me.

He who has an ear, hear what the Spirit says unto you. To those who will pay the price, share the pain, persevere and are open to each other, my Father will give his Glory.

A Participant's Response to the Letters to the Churches

As soon as I got back from the Bible Study Week, I started talking about the letter we wrote to the Churches in England, I talked about it to someone from High Street Evangelism who said they'd have it read out at their church. Next I arranged with the Minister to talk at the Baptist church about the week for two minutes and about the letter that we wrote.

After that I went to one of the magazine editors at the Methodist church I attend to try to put it into the church's magazine. At the Baptist church, I spoke about the week then talked about the letter and read it out at the end of my talk.

With the Methodist church magazine deadline due I told one of the editors about the letter then gave someone a copy of it for them to put it in the magazine, but it failed to go in. The editor pulled me to one side and said he wanted to think about it a bit more. That's the last I've heard of it so far.

Christ's analysis of the Seven Churches

Name	**Strengths**	**Barriers**
Ephesus	Works of grace and obedience. Intolerance of evil, applying Apostolic criteria to measure standards. Uncompromising endurance.	Departure from its founding and instituting characteristics and priorities. (Lost first love.)
Smyrna	Able to work on low budget. (Advanced despite poverty.) Understood true values (but you are rich).	Ecomonic poverty. Active opposition. Ministering in the face of counterfeits (synagogue of Satan).
Pergamum	Confessional faith despite threatening evil. (Satan's throne.) Ultimate loyalty in the face of death. (Martyr-Antipas.)	Situated in poor location. (Where throne of Satan is.)
Thyatira	Conscious of social needs (service). Increasing graces (last better than first).	Worthy part of congregation was being diminished by effect of false teaching. Succumbed to its environmental pressures (shared pagan feasts).
Sardis	A nucleus of purity (a few undefiled).	Hypocrisy (not living up to their name). Negligence (need to be watchful). Uncompleted assignments (works not perfect).
Philadelphia	Reliability (kept word and name). Opportunity (open door).	Internal limitations (little strength).
Laodicea	Prosperous (increased in goods).	Indifferent (neither hot nor cold). Ignorance (knoweth not...)

Interventions	**Promises**	**Reservations**
Reflective thought (remember). Corrective measures (repent). Instigate action (renew first love).	Right of access (to tree of life). Future to anticipate (eschatological perspective).	Future prospects depend upon present resolves. (Overcoming is a prerequisite for fulfilled hope).
Since no action is appropriate, a new mind-set is needed, i.e. God is sovereign (I know...).	A divine limitation is set upon the tribulation.	Cannot rely on the past.
Alternative of either: action from within congregation (repent); action from without, (sword of Christ).	Individual nurture (manna). Individual reward (white stone).	Accommodation of minority groups who support false teaching.
Corrective measures (repentance). Radical reforms (cast some out). Place ceiling on expected load-bearing capacity (no further burden).	Authority to administrate affairs (rule). Participation in Christ's glory.	
Regular assessment. Restructuring (strengthen).	Be robed (garment). Be recorded (Book of Life). Be recognized (confessed).	Weakness and incompleteness are a characteristic.
Provide maintenance in affairs (hold fast).	Preservation (I will keep). Permanence (go no more out).	
Counselling offered. Confrontation (give rebuke).	Re-establishment of fellowship (if you open... I will come in).	Their tendency to cause another to vomit can only be offset by a fresh disposition, i.e. zeal.

Interlude

Sheila Mayo

Suffering

Sorrow seems to have accompanied us today.

This morning our prayers were led by three members of the Cherubim and Seraphim Church who helped us worship "with our whole selves", and told of how they would pray and praise on the sea shore, and in the market place. Later, we participated in two Bible study workshops, one from an Orthodox, and one from a Church of God perspective. We were left asking, "How can we respond to the theological discoveries of the Third World and create a new language?"

John's "Revelation" is an inspired synthesis, drawing upon the wealth of symbolism to be found in the Old Testament. All the prophecies once applied to the historic Israel "after the flesh" are now to find their completion in the new, universal people of God; the story of seven small churches, weak, lukewarm, persecuted communities called to be faithful; the myrrh-bearing women, a story of immense courage and inspired ministry when "all had forsook him and fled". On this frail basis began the disclosure of the good news.

Our walk today took us past a slope where tree after tree had been brought to the ground by a hurricane several years ago. The same seemed to be happening to a lot of our pre-conceived ideas, and there wasn't much sign of new growth, as yet. But in the evening we took care of each other in various ways, including table tennis, conversation and foot massage!

Living God, who came to your world and entered human pain
Come and be in every painful place in our lives, in every painful place in our world, today;
Living God who worked in the secret darkness to raise Christ from the grave;
Come and work in every secret dark place of our lives, in every secret dark place of our world today;
Living God who sent women out to proclaim the resurrection to the frightened, imprisoned disciples;
Come and empower us in every frightening, imprisoned place in our lives, in every frightening, imprisoned place in our world today.

Ecumenical Forum of European Christian Women, *Who are you looking for?*

Prelude to Chapters Five and Six

How would you explain "The Word of God" to a ten-year-old child?

Wille Riekkinen

The next day John saw Jesus coming to him, and said: "There is the Lamb of God". (John 1.29)

Do you understand what this means? Already we have touched on the problem of religious language if we try to clarify what we mean by "gospel", "salvation" or "kingdom". I even asked if we should stop talking about kingdom, and use other phrases if we really want to communicate the very message of the Bible today. Already the writers of the Bible reworded the old message. Let's take an example, John 1.1–8. Do you understand what you are reading?

We must begin by reminding ourselves that the original context of Christianity was Jewish, Jesus and the disciples were born Jews and from the start their language was Aramaic. It was not long before "the Church" began to take its message into the Hellenistic world. Now its message has to be proclaimed among people to whom Jewish ideas, for example about the kingdom of God, were foreign and unknown. We might have expected that these foreigners would have been a great handicap to the early Church. However, that was not so. We find that its mission strategy was enormously successful. How could this be when the problems of communication were so great?

The term "Messiah", so central to Jewish thinking, was completely unknown to the Greek. Jesus as "Messiah" would have meant nothing at all. I said before, if we say to youngsters today "Jesus was a High Priest according to the order of Melchizedek" they would simply mutter "So what?" take their walkmans and their bikes and disappear. And we are left alone with our Bibles asking ourselves "How can we present the Christian message in a more meaningful way?"

Tradition tells us that around the year AD 100 there was a Christian in the Greek city of Ephesus in Asia Minor who was fascinated by this very problem. His name was John. John succeeded in finding a symbolic language — everyday words — in order to speak to women and men of his own time and culture. The fact that he was able to do that may encourage us today. "He used words which are as much at home in the rooms of children as in those of mystics" (William Barclay in *Jesus of Nazareth*), and his genius was to speak to his contemporaries not about a Messiah but about "the Word".

Here was a concept to which Jews and Greeks would relate. It may be useful for us to discover the basis of John's strategy by looking at the Jewish and Greek thought about "the Word". What did Jewish people mean by it? And what did it mean to the Greeks?

But before going on to that exercise what do *you* mean when *you* say Jesus is the Word of God? Imagine that *you* have to explain this to a ten-year-old.

So now, let us look at the Jewish context. To Jewish people a word is not merely a sound. It is much more. It has an independent existence. It is an active power which in itself is able to achieve something. "So also will be the word that I speak — it will not fail to do what I plan for it. . ." (Isaiah 55.11).

The Old Testament was written mainly in Hebrew. But by the time of Jesus Jews no longer knew Hebrew very well, they were now speaking Aramaic. In the Aramaic sermons and explanations (called *Targum*) which formed a central part of worship, every effort was made to avoid speaking the whole name "Jahweh" and so they used the expression "Word of God" instead. *Davar* in Hebrew and *logos* in Greek mean "word", "reason", and "light". They personify God's creative power. They are ways to God, means by which the very will of God, justice, is constantly brought to the mind and heart of humankind. Here was the true wisdom of the Wisdom literature, the eternal justice and harmony, the seeking, creating and illuminating power of God. So John could say to the Jewish people, "If you want to discover the Word of God look at Jesus. In him the wisdom of God came amongst you."

And how could the Greeks understand it? In Greek thought the idea of "the Word" was already present and it had originated in the same town in which the fourth gospel was written. About 650 years before John there lived a philosopher called Heraclitus whose basic principle was that everything in this world is constantly changing. His best known illustration is that no one can step more than once into the same river because the water that flows in it today is not the same water that flowed there yesterday. For Heraclitus everything in the world was like that, in a state of flux. Why then, you might ask, did the water continue to flow? Why did it not stop? Why is life not complete chaos? His answer was that all this change was controlled by the *Logos*, the Reason of God, the principle of order by which the cosmos continues to exist.

Because of "the *Logos*" nothing moves with aimless feet. John could have said to Heraclitus and some Stoic philosophers after him, as well as to the Hellenistic Jews of Alexandria, that "The *Logos* signifies nothing less than the mind of God which controls all. For centuries you have been talking about the *Logos*, the power by which the world is ordered, the power by which human beings think, reason and recognize truth and justice." So this creating, illuminating, controlling, harmony — and justice-seeking, peace-furthering and sustaining mind of God has come to earth in Jesus, proclaimed the early Church. "The Word became a human being and, full of grace and truth, lived among us. We saw his glory, the glory which he received as the Father's only Son." (John 1.14).

So, what does this mean in the circumstances of your daily lives, in the diversity of situations in which we find our world today? Do these words which illustrate the biblical concept of that word—wisdom, reason, light, truth, justice, peace, harmony, creation—form that basic motivation for us as Christians? If so we are already following him who demonstrated these things 2000 years ago in a deeply challenging way.

Chapter Five

The Healing of Naaman

(2 Kings 5.1–14)

Bill Denning

Bill Denning organizes groups and conferences through the Creative Art Network, Maypole Farm, near Bristol, UK. Included with this session are some of his notes on leading workshops and Bible studies.

Introduction

As an "ice-breaker" the group engaged in a number of exercises:

- Exploring reactions to "being creative" (fear of failure, etc.). Sitting in a circle with candle and flowers — symbols of creativity and God's presence.
- Relaxation exercises to get warm in a cool room and to get in touch with our bodies.

Then, entering into the role of characters in the story, the group explored the feelings of:

- The little slave girl, with no name, torn from her home (fear, confusion, anger).
- Naaman, the powerful commander with leprosy (fear, anger, and disgust).

Creation

With a brief practical explanation about using art forms available, the group worked *individually* and in *silence* using paint, clay, or writing in an atmosphere of creative stillness. Imagination was stirred by asking the group to identify:

- Images
- Feelings
- Persons in the text

As people finished, those who wished, talked together and shared experiences, in twos and threes.

Reflection

The group shared the experience of the creativity of other members of the group, inviting responses to one another's work, with an opportunity for the artists to comment on their own. Specific questions then followed, all linked to the experience of members of the group:

- What did Naaman need to let go of, to find healing?
- Who for you, is the key person in the healing?
- What were the identifiable stages in the healing process?

  Issues that confront us in the text:

  Race
  Power
  Wealth
  Health
  Sexism
  War

Lord Jesus
Son of the living God
call us into deeper and more demanding fellowship
with one another and with you.
Help us to reach beyond
our self will and self preservation
our longing for recognition and achievement
and to offer you only a humble mind
that knows it can do nothing without you
for your Glory's sake. Amen.

John V Taylor

Creativity Workshops: some Notes for Leaders

Creativity workshops need a good structure to work within, where people know the boundaries of time and so on, but total freedom and exploration are encouraged, and the outcome cannot be known beforehand. The broad *three-stage* pattern shown here may well have linking stages, or in-between happenings, like meals for instance, or free time. These are indicated here between the main sections of "induction", "creation", and "reflection". While the whole three-stage process could be completed in 1½ hours, it really needs more, with a break between "creation" and "reflection" if the latter is going to extend on into worship.

The "introduction" section is only done once, and where several workshops are anticipated, then the "reflection" session is designed to lead into, and open up the next "creation" perhaps using a different art form. But the theme starts to branch out once reflection begins, and a natural follow-on becomes obvious.

Induction

This should begin with meeting one another, learning names, and splitting into smaller groups if this is necessary. A secure framework for the session should then be given, offering the ground rules of the process, the aim of the event, and the times and places where things will happen. The final part of the induction process is to do a few warm-up exercises, some drama, or games, etc., to free the atmosphere. However, a "way out with honour" must be provided for those who simply cannot or will not participate. Laughter, movement and closeness are the aims of this warm-up time. This section is very important as it is not easy to draw out creativity from a cold start.

Creation

Use as much silence as possible. Move away from words into images and feelings, using colour, clay, poetry, music making, drama, dance, etc.

Follow this with coffee or a meal or a time for sharing with one another.

Reflection

A time for sharing insights: affirming and listening to one another and to what God is saying. Then accepting and or celebrating these things.

Chapter Six

Justice, Peace and the Integrity of Creation

Jeni Parsons

Dr Jeni Parsons was Director of Studies for The Aston Training Scheme, a pre-college preparation course for men and women who will be entering the Anglican ministry. She is now in training for the ordained ministry at Westcott House, Cambridge. The theme of healing was strongly heard in this workshop; not only the healing of individual women or men but the healing of the earth: "We must in spite of all difficulties and disappointments sustain our efforts to change entrenched and destructive situations. Better to light a candle than to curse the darkness" (Jurgen Moltmann, "The Disarming Child" in The Power of the Powerless).

Method

The method used in this study comes from an American, Walter Wink, and a further development of the theory and practice of the questioning method can be found in his book *Transforming Bible Study*, (2nd edition, Mowbray, 1990). The method adopted here involves the asking of "beginners' questions" and thereby integrates the participants' experience with the text so that each speaks to the other. In this way neither the text nor the experiences dominate but both are brought together in a way that allows each to critique the other. It is also a method that honours the experience and skill of each participant for it does not give priority to only one type of knowledge or expertise but allows everyone to participate as equals. The method encourages the participants to "become as little children" in the simplicity of their questions because we all know that the simple or obvious question usually goes to the heart of the matter! Each participant should feel free to speak or not as they wish. This method is not to facilitate the producing of a common mind on any issue and the leader should not look for the submission of any individual to another viewpoint. Dialogue is a key word! Leaders need not work slavishly through all the questions in a section nor use them in the order in which they appear here if they feel another strategy would work as well, however, the author has tried to move from human experience to the text and back again as she has framed the questions and there is a logic to the order as it is set.

Setting the Room

Put the number of chairs required in a circle so that everyone has an equal place. Place the Bible open in the centre of the circle to remind participants that it is the Bible which they are addressing. Although the leader initially seems prominent in this method, the text is the hub and the participants' contributions radiate from it like the spokes of a wheel. Each participant needs to have a photocopy of the portion of text to be studied and a pen so that they can write on their copy. The leader of the study is not the centre of attention in this method but is there to move the discussion along at appropriate points by introducing another question when needed.

Pattern of the Session

- Group dialogue around some "beginners' questions"
- Reflection alone and then in the group
- Action and artistic expression
- Reflection on the experience of the study in the group

Beginning the Session

- Prayer

  Holy Spirit open us to the text,
  To listening to one another,
  To listening to ourselves,
  To looking outward at God's world.
  We ask this of our God;
  the God of Abraham, Isaac and Jacob,
  of Sarah, Rebekah, Rachel and Jesus. Amen.
- Spend a little time making sure the group members have a chance to say their names and how they are feeling so that the group can begin to feel comfortable with one another. If this is the first time they have met then this will need to take a more extended form as the leader sees fit.

- The Bible in the centre is opened to the portion of the text for the session and someone reads the text aloud whilst the participants listen attentively. When the reading is finished allow a few minutes for the participants to mark on their copies of the text any points that puzzle, surprise, or irritate them. Then the text is read again with the participants following carefully on their copies marking anything else that catches their eye.

The Study

(The method here can be used for any passage but the questions are cast with Exodus 23 in mind. Wink, in his book, gives questions for use with gospel passages but almost any part of the Bible can be illuminated by the careful framing of questions along the lines of the ones suggested here.)

Exodus 23.1–19

The text has been divided into three parts and it is possible to take just one part for a single study and to return to the other two parts on another occasion. The book of Exodus is perhaps the most important book in the whole Bible because from it have come many of the important themes of Judaism and Christianity— themes of liberation; of being the people of God; of justice, peace and the integrity of creation; of making a covenant; of the law of God; of the Ten Commandments; of being brought out of the land of Egypt; of wandering in the desert, and so on.

Some Questions for Exodus 23.1–9

- What is your most recent personal experience of injustice?
- What status do those who perpetuate injustice have?
- Who are we unjust towards?
- What sort of community lies behind these rules for justice in Exodus 23?
- Why must people be just according to Exodus 23?
- What sort of God calls them to this in this text?
- What other beginners' questions do you have on this section of text?
- What, if anything, do you want to say about this section of text using your reactions to hearing the text read?

Some Questions for Exodus 23.10–13

- Where does the pattern of Sabbath rest come from?
- Who is it for?
- How do you use your rest time?
- How is resting important for human beings and for nature?
- How is rest a part of harmony in the world?
- What is peace for you in this context of rest and recreation?
- How does this peace you value relate to justice?
- What other beginners' questions do you have on this section of text?
- What, if anything, do you want to say about this section of text using your reactions to hearing the text read?

Some Questions for Exodus 23.14–19

- What festivals are being described here?
- What do they commemorate?
- What themes are they about?
- Are there Christian festivals that speak to you about these things?
- What other beginners' questions do you have on this section of text?
- What, if anything, do you want to say about this section of text using your reactions to hearing the text read?

Reflection

- Alone, each participant spends a few minutes thinking about the text they have just entered into dialogue with and draws any images that come to mind either from the text, from the discussion or from how they are feeling.
- In twos, discuss feelings and insights from the drawing and the study.
- The whole group express their experience in a collage which need not be discussed in advance but can be constructed together as they go along by sharing images and insights. The collage can become a meditation on the work of the group. During the collage making it can be appropriate to play some taped music to encourage participants to maintain a thoughtful and reflective mood even though they will need to talk softly with one another.

- When the collage is complete, reassemble the group for reflection together on the experience of studying Exodus 23.1–19, of working artistically and of sharing together.

Interlude

Sheila Mayo

Lord, you invite us to your feast
and we accept
In the name of Jesus. Amen.

That was our breakfast grace; but we were to be "graced" in other ways today. With the vivid image of "the tree of life" we set out for our two workshops, one on the Healing of Naaman, the other on Justice, Peace and the Integrity of Creation.

> *Is it not strange that an infant should be the heir of the whole world, and see these mysteries which the books of the learned never unfold?*
>
> Thomas Traherne, *Centuries*

These were two workshops "costing not less than everything". Asking us to shed our defences; work together with unfamiliar materials— colour, cloth, clay, with underlying themes of healing, healing of the individual wounded body and psyche; healing of the body and psyche of our broken world.

> *We also shed ideas of perfection. Jesus could not have known this word. In Matthew 5.48 the Aramaic "Shalom" or "Tamim" means whole, entire, completed. And the goal of our Christian life becomes not enlightment but wholeness; and acceptance of this muddled bundle of experiences as a possible theatre of God's creative work.*
>
> Rowan Williams, *The Wound of Knowledge*

Picasso painted a famous portrait of Gertrude Stein. After 80 sittings at which he had painted and repainted her face he wiped it away. When winter came he stopped painting: in the spring he returned to his canvas. Without his model and in a few moments he painted in a face which is evocative, more than life like, the epitome of Gertrude Stein.

We learnt to see with the eyes of a child today, "if the doors of perception were cleansed, everything would appear to man as it is, infinite. For man has closed himself up till he sees all things through the narrow chinks of his cavern" (William Blake).

Wille had asked us about "translating" words and concepts; forming a new language. The words and concepts we use in religious language are pious memorials for pious men and women who were able to crystallize as it were from the collective unconscious of tribe and nation those symbols which "spoke" to society as a whole.

Are these images arising in our culture today? We are living through the dark night of our institutions as well as that of our own spirits. In the darkness, in the silence we are in quest of a new myth. Has Christianity in it the power to recreate symbols which speak, breathe, and empower us for our life and work today?

They will reveal a Christ who moves incognito through the crowds of men and women; a Christianity which receives its new identity from the lands of strangers certainly of other races and also of other faiths.

Perhaps humankind has to go through its childhood and its adolescence before it can come to creative maturity. Perhaps we had to let this adolescent period, which we now call the Enlightenment, carry us to the brink of nuclear holocaust before — staring extinction in the face — we could wake up to our own divine and demonic powers of creativity.

Loving God
We pray for all those living with HIV, or AIDS
For those they love, their families and friends.
We thank you for all the good things they have discovered:
For the joy of friendship and love, mutual support and care,
And we ask that with them, we may come to know ourselves
As lovely in your sight
Through Christ our Lord. Amen.

Prayer from Southwark
Cathedral

Prelude to Chapters Seven and Eight

Then we all sat down

Wille Riekkinen

When we meet like this we experience "formation for mission". Christians *are* mission, and those of us who have no sense of commitment to mission are like salt which has lost its saltiness. But when you ask "What is this mission?" there is hardly any agreement at all. But let's try!

Mission can mean "proclamation", "making disciples". It can mean "participation" in God's commitment to the work of liberation, both personal and social, so that our God can be seen to be "Lord of all creation".

So mission must be seen "holistically" and as our common responsibility, not just the responsibility of a mission society or of a few people called "missionaries". Mission is the responsibility of the people of God. But who are they? Us! So, what are our responsibilities and what are our gifts for this work?

Mission takes place everywhere, everywhere: on factory floors in Liverpool, in shops in central London, on the beach in Devon, in a school bus in Nottingham, on a training camp in Wimbledon, or in a Bible study workshop in Dunford House. Wherever there are people, there is the possibility for mission. And this mission is spreading not only from England to India, or from Germany to Africa, from Finland to Guatemala, but it's here, it's there, everywhere we meet people. Where there are people there is the place of mission. Mission is people. It means to take earnestly the words in Revelation 21.3 where the prophet says to us: "Now God's home is with human beings! He will live with them, and they shall be his people".

How else can this "good news" become real unless mission is begun in and through us? To do this job we need each other, women and men. What kind of people should we then be? Small living stones or steady rocks like St Peter? If you feel just like a small stone, don't worry, just go on. Even so-called heroes like Peter were only human beings like us.

So, today let us focus on Peter. Try to learn from him. His original name was Simon, but Jesus gave him another name. The Aramaic name for "rock", *Cephas*, which is in Greek *Petros*. This nickname tells us about Peter's function — to be solid, reliable, a leader in the congregation and in the early Church. He was a fisherman, not sophisticated, but practical. His family came from Bethsaida of Galilee, and he had a home in Jesus' town, Capernaum, where he lived with his family. He figures personally in the gospels, always taking the initiative and acting as the spokesman for the disciples. When Jesus asked them their opinion of his own identity, it was of course Peter who answered.

Matthew 16.13–23
Here we see a deep conflict in Peter. A man of extreme opinions. The ultimate optimist, a man of God and as a weak witness, a typical human being at the same time. The first to defend Jesus in Gethsemane. The most prominent one to deny him later.

Luke 22.59–62
In what ways do we defend or deny Jesus?
How is he revealed in our personal life every day?

Matthew 14.12–26, John 13.1–10, 21–25
So, the whole time keep the figure of Peter in your mind. Let us now commemorate the last supper.

It is usual to picture Jesus and his friends behind a long table as in the famous painting by Leonardo da Vinci. It is a nice picture, but he has set it in sixteenth-century Italy. As such, it is a very good example of how we tend to interpret the Bible from our own, that is in this case, Western perspective.

But archaeological and historical evidence makes it clear that in ancient times tables were arranged for feast-needs in U-shapes with places for ten to thirteen people around each. So, I have numbered the places 1 to 13 and, just to make it very concrete I would like to invite thirteen of you to the table. Feel free, choose a place and sit down; and those who don't come choose a place and imagine you are sitting there!

Now, let us imagine we have here Jesus and twelve disciples, but who is who? It is still a secret! First let's read John 13.1–10, 21–26, from there we can identify some figures at the table. First, let's say that this is nothing personal. If you happen to be Jesus or Judas, or Peter, or John, it doesn't matter.

So, to help us identify these figures I am using a reconstruction by Dr Peter Fleming from Jerusalem. You remember, Jesus was the host and he had sent Peter and John to prepare everything for supper.

So Jesus sat here, No. 2, with two important guests, the host with one on his right hand and the other on his left (Matthew 20.20–21). They sat where best friends always sat and used the same dipping bowl. (You see, there are four bowls placed amongst the guests and special guests sat along the left wing of the U-table.) If you have read your Bible carefully you will know where John sat, reclining on his left elbow, eating with his right hand and leaning on Jesus. So where is he? One might expect that Jesus would give place No. 1 to Peter, John or James as they seemed to be the closest circle of his friends and actually he did so, he gave the place No. 1 to John, his favourite disciple.

What about Judas? We know the place at the left-hand side of the host was the place of the guest of honour, and we see two indications here. One: there was the custom of offering a piece of meat ("the sop") to the guest of honour. So Jesus took it and gave it to the one who not only received it, but with whom Jesus was reclining throughout the meal. Who was he? It is evident that Judas was in the place No. 3, close enough to Jesus to be eating from the same dishes (John 13.25).

So Jesus was trying to show Judas special sensitivity as part of the group, even until the very end. And as Judas found it impossible to reconcile Jesus' behaviour with his messianic role, this must have strengthened the conflict in his heart, because he had already decided to hand Jesus over to the Romans.

Now, we still have to find the place for Peter. Where can he be? He needed to be near John to ask who the betrayer would be without the others hearing him. So his place must have been somewhere ... here (on the right wing of the U-table).

Before deciding, let's look at Peter's behaviour. Luke tells us that there was a dispute as to who was the greater as they walked into the guest chamber (Luke 22.29), and it seems to me that this rivalry was, and is still rather common. Probably Peter and John both imagined that they would be sitting either side of Jesus. It may have been that impetuous Peter, in an "I'll show you" attitude, stamped over to the least seat (No. 13) usually reserved for slaves and servants. You will remember when Peter protested to Jesus previously, "Never at any time will you wash my feet!" and then changed it to "not my feet only, but my hands and my head as well".

So here is all-or-nothing Peter. Not very different from us: impetuous selfish, a strong leader, a denier, unsure, weak, and an idealistic human being. In him the extremes meet. No wonder tradition points out that he was, after preaching in Rome, crucified head downwards near the Tiber city.

Slowly he had been transformed to be a missionary, a charismatic leader, spokesperson in the early Church. And as such he had a tremendous job — one meant for all Christians.

John 21.15–19
Now you can forget your role at this table.

Nobody is Judas, Jesus, John or Peter or any of the others. You are who you are. We are who we are. Followers of Jesus today.

But still, think about the passage we just read. It's interesting: Peter was not asked for his qualities, but "Do you love me?" And he got a tremendous job to do! Now we have the same job to do, with all the gifts given to us.

If we look at ourselves we might be afraid, because of the kind of people we are. Be sure, God's spirit will help us to know the truth, the way, the life and help us to participate in this mission, proclaim this gospel, bringing salvation to those we meet, extending the Kingdom.

Let's stay for a few moments in silence. "How was Peter? How am I?"

A Participant's Response

Watching Wille lay the table for the Last Supper was an experience which stays in my mind from the Bible Study Week above most others. Arranging tables in a horseshoe and placing dipping bowls with care, he numbered the places from one to thirteen. Jesus' place was the first he told us about because custom at that time sat the host near the left end of the horseshoe. Next came John leaning, as custom was, against Jesus' breast in the place of the special friend. Peter was on the opposite side of the horseshoe, able to converse with Jesus because he had taken up the servant's place and was therefore in eye-line.

The other participants at the Bible Study Week were as intrigued as I was listening to Wille's gentle yet incisive explanation and we were moved as he invited us visually to participate in one of the central Christian stories. But the final point he was to show us that morning concerned the person who shared the dipping bowl with John and Jesus:

> *After Jesus had said this, he was deeply troubled and declared openly, "I am telling you the truth: one of you is going to betray me."*
>
> *The disciples looked at one another, completely puzzled about whom he meant. One of the disciples, the one whom Jesus loved, was sitting next to Jesus. Simon Peter motioned to him and said, "Ask him whom he is talking about."*

So that disciple moved closer to Jesus' side and asked, "Who is it, Lord?"

Jesus answered, "I will dip some bread in the sauce and give it to him; he is the man." So he took a piece of bread, dipped it, and gave it to Judas, the son of Simon Iscariot.

The implication became plain to us all, Judas was the man next to Jesus the host, whom Jesus would have been resting against — Judas was the man in the seat of the special guest. It occurred to me that in placing Judas there Jesus laid himself open in vulnerability to love and to attack, for it would have been the best seat for an assassin with the unprotected back of Jesus exposed to his right hand. Was this the significance of the seat of the guest of honour that the host placed himself at his mercy and thereby showed complete trust? At this point I didn't hear any more of Wille's explanation or reflection because my mind was completely taken up with images of trust and vulnerability, of temptation and duty. I wondered whether John, the only other person Jesus could have reached with the morsel, was afraid it might be him who would betray him because of the intensity of his love? (So many questions and fragments whirled round in my thoughts and then, at last, I was back with Wille's Finnish accented English talking of Jesus.)

Chapter Seven

Casual Labourers

(Matthew 20.1–15)

Alison Norris

Alison Norris has worked for the last thirteen years with the South London Industrial Mission, in Southwark, England, and now works for the Overseas Division of the Methodist Church. She has always been primarily concerned with what people who are marginalized from the mainstream of society know about God. When she was a prison chaplain she says she learnt more theology in prison that outside!

Outline of Session:

Introduction to explain aim and process

Exploring our experience (how is the Gospel "heard"?)

Setting the scene (an imaginary guided tour of the people in the market square):

- Questions to the groups
- Jesus tells the story
- Practical application

Introduction

This session relies on getting under the skin of the characters in Jesus' parable of the workers in the vineyard.

Participants divide into four groups: the landless day labourers, local landowners, poor tenant farmers, and a group of women. A profile of each of these groups is given to help people into their roles; the scene is set, and then the parable is read. After the parable is read, each group is asked a series of questions which they must answer among themselves. Each of the four group's answers are then shared with the whole group and applications for today sought.

Group Role Outlines

Landless Day Labourers (Group 1)

You are a group of landless day labourers. You live by getting casual labour in the surrounding farms and houses as best you can. Some of you may have a small plot to grow a few vegetables, or you may have some skill, e.g. as a tinker or wheelwright, or you may have one or two goats which can be grazed on the hills some distance from the village — your wife or children will go with them.

The way you get work is to come here into the town centre early in the morning to wait for the local farmers and farm foremen who come in, especially at this time of year (harvest) to hire additional labour.

You know that the Law says that you must be paid a fixed wage, and that it must be paid to you each day, but not all the local employers are scrupulous in observing this law — some may try to make you work a piece rate for example.

Today some of you have succeeded in getting work, and some have not.

Local Landowners (Group 2)

You are a group of local landowners and farmers. Your farms vary in size from one or two orange groves or small vineyards, to large farms some of which may be occupied by tenant farmers.

Some of you may well live here all the year round, perhaps going up to Jerusalem for major festivals; some of you may only be here at the moment because it is harvest time, and you wish to oversee the harvesting, sale and storage of your crops.

Some of you may well be "working farmers", accustomed to doing most of the work yourselves, and employing only one or two regular workers. But all of you will be dependent at harvest time on a supply of casual labour, which you will employ by coming yourselves, or sending your foreman if you have one, to the town square early in the morning to hire as many men as you can.

You know that the Law says that you must pay a standard daily rate of pay to all hired labourers, and that this must always be paid at the end of each day. But you may not be sure that all of you actually observe this law.

Poor Tenant Farmers (Group 3)
You are a group of poor tenant farmers. You hold your usually small pieces of land from large landowners, many of you have never actually seen your landlords who live on the coast, or in the mountains of Lebanon. They send a land agent once a year to collect the rent, and that is about all. You are basically subsistence farmers, though your family may make a little extra cash through sewing or washing work, or through some skill or trade.

At this time of year (harvest) there is a great deal of work to do in harvesting and storing, even selling if there is a surplus. You really need all your family members to work your own piece of land, but often it is just at this time that you are also pressed to work on the landlord's farms. This can be particularly difficult if you do not have a large family.

Sometimes you are able to get a neighbour whose crop is already in to help you; at other times you must go down to the town to hire casual labour from the market place, like the other farmers and landowners in the area. You know that there is a fixed daily wage laid down in the Law, and that this must be paid in the evening of the day of work; but unless you have surplus to sell in the market place you do not have any ready cash to pay.

A Group of Women (Group 4)
You are a group of women, the wives and daughters and mothers of some of the local farmers and day labourers. If your husbands are tenant farmers or labourers with some small garden plot, then you will be responsible for growing at least some of the family food; very few of you will have access to private water, so some at least of your work will be bringing water from the town's wells, or taking clothes for washing to the river.

You and your children may also be responsible for pasturing animals on the hills which are common grazing land, some distance from the town. Your husband or sons may also have some trade such as tinkering or thatching which can be plied in the town to bring in extra cash.

Today some of your husbands/sons/fathers may have found work by going to the town centre in the early morning in the hope of being hired to bring in the harvest on some of the farms around the town. You know that the Law says that there is a fixed daily wage, and that this should be paid on the same day, but you also know that not all the local farmers observe this law. Nobody has ever paid *you* for a day's labour in your life!

Setting the Scene

We are in a small country town in Judea. It is harvest time, and this year there is a good harvest.

It is evening; it has been a very hot day, and now that the cool time is here you have all gathered in the town square to relax — to gossip; to get a legal opinion on that matter of your neighbour's wall which has fallen down all over your best squash plants; to look over the young men, as it really is time you were finding a husband for your daughter; to drink a cup of wine and forget the troubles of the day.

The smells of bread have given way to the smell of the goats as they make their way back from a day's grazing on the hills. The cooking and sweat, the crying and shouting of the day are beginning to fade into the cool and quiet of the night.

There is tiredness in your bodies after a hard day's work, but your minds are filled with thoughts, questions, ideas.

(At this point participants are invited to take on their various roles.)

On this occasion you also have in the town a wandering rabbi called Jesus who comes from Nazareth, you've heard. There are quite a lot of these wandering bands around these days, people who have given up all semblance of a sensible, settled home life, and follow some guru around, in the belief that he is the Messiah, or a new prophet or some such thing. Some of you have heard this one preaching before, and he talks a lot about what he calls "the Kingdom of God".

You have heard him say that the Kingdom of God is amongst us. Not that you see a lot of evidence of it. What is it, this Kingdom of God? (and is there anything in it for you?)

(Read and tell the story (Matthew 20.1–15).)

You may also like to consider and discuss this contemporary situation:

- This system still actually operates in the Gaza Strip where Israeli employers come each day to pick up casual labourers.

Questions for all the Groups to Discuss

- What are the major concerns and problems of your life?
- What do you hope for in life?
- What kind of a day have you had today?

Jesus Tells the Story

- What did the different groups hear? Was it the same or different?
- Why did they react in that way?
- What do you think that Jesus was saying to them?
- What was Matthew saying?

Application

- Discuss similar situations in your country today.
- Describe similar groups in our society and churches.
- For whom is this story good news?
- Can you write a parable for our time?

Chapter Eight

The Sale of the Vineyard

(1 Kings 21.1–16)

Paul Bates

Paul Bates is a Canon of Westminster Abbey, a place of pilgrimage; significant in the life of the British nation with its strong links with other denominations and faiths. This workshop proved to be creative and disturbing. Perhaps it asked us to move from an insular national theology to one more global, less restricted in its boundaries, and to move from preaching to dialogue.

Introduction

Begin by stating that half of the Bible consists of stories, and that, if we are to fully grasp the meaning of those stories for ourselves, our neighbours and our society, we must place ourselves within the stories. It is important not to impose our understanding of "what a story means" on others. Let each one of us try to find out for ourselves.

Setting the Scene

The clash between the traditional values of the past and the values of a modern culture is not new. It has been going on for a long time. The story of Naboth and his vineyard can be interpreted at that level.

Divide into three groups. Each group takes the part of one of the characters in the story of Naboth. Read the short brief on what they might have believed, and then prepare to explain why you acted as you did. (There is a short dramatisation of the scenario at the end of the chapter.)

Naboth

Your vineyard has been handed down from your family. It is your duty to leave it in good condition when the time comes for you to pass it down to your son. You are responsible for it, but not in control of it. Even the King has no right to it, because the King too is under the same Law which comes from God. Holding your vineyard in trust gives you meaning, and a place in the story of your family.

Ahab
Everything can be bought and sold, and the King has the right to the first pickings. You are not cheating Naboth but offering him a good price. You are dimly aware that you too are under the Law of God, because although you don't like the fact that Naboth has refused you, you are prepared to respect his resistance.

Jezebel
You are a Canaanite, and can't understand what all the fuss is about. You come from another culture where the King can do anything he wants, where land is a commodity which *can be obtained by any means at all,* and where the King does not come under the same Law as everyone else. The way in which this funny society of Israel runs things blocks change and inventiveness. So you are prepared to do anything to get what you want because you believe that is right, even if it means using the Law as a tool to serve your own interest.

For the Groups to Discuss

Say what you want to say to the other two groups, and let a discussion develop.

Topics to Stimulate Discussion
When one culture comes into contact with another, what happens? Was Naboth's profound belief that the vineyard belonged to God, given to his family as part of God's covenant with God's people, a strange religious quirk? Could the up-to-date Jezebel ignore his culture because her own did not recognize the values of his? And what of Ahab, caught between the two?

Today, what people believe in seems to be conditioned mainly by the surrounding culture. Christian groups or sects that try to resist the culture are frequently dismissed as cranks or freaks. In British society, the group who are struggling most obviously with the issue is the Muslim community. In Iran, the issue is being tackled in a traditional way, and is proving an affront to Western values. How should a faithful Muslim react in this country? It is, perhaps, an indication of the way in which modern values have eaten away at the traditional Christian ones that the obvious example of the clash between the old and the new should come from a different faith.

Divide into Pairs
As modern Ahabs, caught between the values of Naboth and the values of Jezebel, where do you feel the conflicts? List the three major ones.

Within the Whole Group
Share lists, and discuss the similarities and differences.

For Prayer

O God, the protector of all that trust in thee, without whom nothing is strong, nothing is holy; Increase and multiply upon us thy mercy; that, thou being our ruler and guide, we may so pass through things temporal, that we finally lose not the things eternal: Grant this, O heavenly Father, for Jesus Christ's sake our Lord.

(*Book of Common Prayer*)

Some Background Information to the Story

The clash of empires — Who shall take the place of Assyria?

Josiah	640–609	Assyrian decline
Jehoahaz	609	Take to Egypt
Jehoiakim	609–598	Revolt against Babylon
Jehoiachin (Coniah)	598/7	First deportation
Zedekiah (uncle)	597–587	Fall of Jerusalem 587

A Scenario from the Story

AHAB: Jez old girl! This is frightfully good, this *Côtes de Jordan.*
JEZEBEL: You know where it comes from, don't you. I look out there every day and think wouldn't it be lovely to turn it into a garden and have parties on our own lawn instead of all this

traipsing around. It's such nonsense not having it, just because Naboth won't sell — and you've offered him top whack.
AHAB: (*picks up telephone*) Hello, Naboth, I'm making you my last offer; you what? You won't sell. . .your inheritance. . .really. . .
JEZEBEL: Ahab, are you king or aren't you?
AHAB: (*aside*) The way things are going these days I'm beginning to wonder myself if I'm in charge any more. . .
JEZEBEL: You haven't even touched your lunch.
AHAB: I've had enough — I'll go and have a lie down.
JEZEBEL: Don't worry, darling, I'll join you in a minute.
AHAB: Where are you going Jez?
JEZEBEL: I'm going to make Naboth an offer he can't refuse. "You cannot hear me as a stranger so I must ask you as a queen."

Lord give us more than pity
give us a passionate reverence
that will redeem pity
by understanding
that there is more than one hunger
a hunger for bread
a hunger for love
a hunger to be allowed to love
this it is that gives us meaning
and the hunger for meaning is the greatest hunger of all

John V Taylor

"To love anyone is nothing else than to wish that person good."

Thomas Aquinas, *Summa Theologia*

Interlude

Sheila Mayo

We have been grounded — earthed. Today is our last day together. We have had such a short time to get to know each other; we came from so many different backgrounds and cultures; now we go back to the pleasures and problems of the life we left.

On our walk today we "beat the bounds". We noticed how the barbed wire fence was interwoven with young green withies.

We have been thinking of boundaries today. Those between the little oasis which was Naboth's vineyard and the gardens of King Ahab. Those between the landless peasants and their employers in the Gaza Strip. Those between the men and the women in the story of the casual labourers. "It's no fun waiting around all day to be valued."

Driving into Chichester in the rain that afternoon the contrast between parking problems, wet shoppers and wailing children, and the austere beauty of the cathedral struck us. It was not until, away from the soaring arches and the awesome tapestry of Graham Sutherland, we came to the Lady Chapel that we found the pilgrims' crosses, scratched into the wall, hundreds of years ago, by other unknowns.

Without looking back, you want to follow Christ: here and now, in the present moment, turn to God and trust in the Gospel. In so doing, you draw from the sources of jubilation.

You think you do not know how to pray. Yet the Risen Christ is there; he loves you before you love him. By "his Spirit who dwells in our hearts," he intercedes in you far more than you imagine.

Even without recognizing him, learn to wait for him with or without words, during long silences when nothing seems to happen. There obsessive discouragements vanish, and creative impulses well up. Nothing can be built up in you without this adventure — finding him in the intimacy of a personal encounter. No one can do it for you.

When you have trouble understanding what he wants of you, tell him so. In the course of daily activities, at every moment, tell him all, even things you cannot bear.

Do not compare yourself with others, and with what they can do. Why wear yourself out regretting what is impossible for you? Could you have forgotten God? Turn to him. No matter what happens, dare to begin over and over again.

Epilogue

Sheila Mayo

A lovely, old, pink, painted home; trees of every kind, set in green pastures; birds of many kinds around you — blackbirds and thrushes and pheasants in pairs; good food to fill you, and all enjoyed amongst pleasant company! All this for starters; what other pleasures could you want? Here in the month of May, at Dunford House we have encountered the myrrh-bearing women, revered in the Greek Orthodox Church, set in icons, and sweet music, and gifts and rejection in the house of Simon.

We have seen the healing of Naaman in the clear river Jordan through the gentle persuasion of a little slave girl; and the joy of painting, collage, modelling in clay and poetry making as we felt freely inspired to create.

We have struggled to play snap as in the children's game, finding Bible stories to snap, but not so easy a game to play. We followed the hard life of those born to be disciples of Jesus, without food or money, only the clothes they stood up in, and a load of work as they went homeless on their way. We have thought of the deep wisdom in the challenges given to the journeying people of God in Exodus, and the little groups of Christians scattered about Asia Minor addressed in the mysterious letters recorded by John in the Book of Revelation "to the angel of the church of ... write ... "

Their burdens fit ours. So many wonderful teachers have directed our minds, so many new friendships made, so much deep discussion, so much laughter, and even more prayers to sustain us.

We have all been changed since we came in through the door. Many of us were looking for certainties in the stories which we could live by; instead we have learned to "live with the stories".

God never says you should have come yesterday;
He never says you must come again tomorrow,
but today if you will hear his voice,
today he will hear you.
He brought light out of darkness,
not out of lesser light;
He can bring thy summer out of winter,
though thou have no spring.
All occasions invite his mercies,
and all times are his season.

John Donne

Appendix

Learning Styles

Some Notes for Group Leaders

In a rapidly changing world established patterns and procedures quickly become outdated. The importance of changing and adapting, and of learning from experience, is increasingly recognized. In recent years there has been considerable development in the understanding of how adults learn through experience.

Learning from experience can be seen as a process, with a number of stages or phases in it. Most models see four essential phases. One of the simplest describes the learning process in four words:

DO — LOOK — THINK — CHANGE

A widely used four-phase model of learning from experience looks like this:

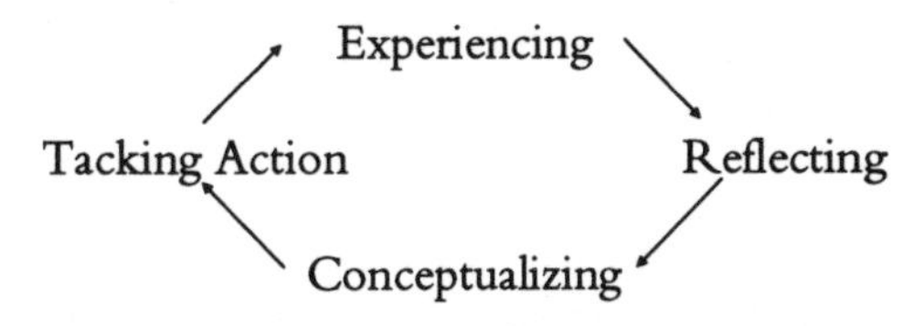

Experiencing includes seeing, hearing, thinking, feeling.
Reflecting includes noting things that seem significant, questioning why things happened this way.
Conceptualizing includes working out explanations, using ideas to "make sense" of observations and reflections, developing general principles.
Taking action includes testing out the implications, using new approaches, making active experiments.
Two points need to be noted:
a. It is a *cycle*: action taken leads to new consequences and new experience and the cycle is repeated.
b. The *phases* are in a logical order, but in practice there is a very great deal of moving backwards and forwards between them.

Learning Abilities

David A Kolb and Ronald Fry of the Massachusetts Institute of Technology, in a paper "Towards an Applied Theory of Experiential Learning", underline the point that "the experiential learning model emphasizes that learning and change result from the *integration* of the emotional experiences with cognitive processes: conceptual analysis and understanding."

They focus on four different kinds of learning abilities required:

- concrete experience abilities — ability to involve oneself fully, openly and without bias
- reflective observation abilities — ability to observe and reflect on these experiences from any perspective
- abstract conceptualization abilities — ability to develop concepts to integrate observations in logically sound theories
- active experimentation abilities — ability to use theories to make decisions and solve problems

Preferred Learning Styles

Peter Honey and Alan Mumford have devised a questionnaire to explore learning styles and have focused on the difference in the ways in which people prefer to learn. They suggest there are four preferred learning styles which correspond to the phases of the experiential learning cycle: activist, reflector, theorist, and pragmatist. The questionnaire is copyright and can be obtained from Peter Honey and Alan Mumford of Ardingly House, 10 Lindon Avenue, Maidenhead, Berks, SL6 6HB. Many people engaged in adult education have found it very stimulating to do the questionnaire and discover their own preferred learning style.

As *learners* we each have our preferred learning style.

As *providers* our tendency is to provide learning opportunities for others in the learning style that suits us without realizing that is what we are doing. We need to provide a variety of learning activities for people of different learning preferences.

This also emphasizes the value of learning together in a group, in which the different learning style preferences of all the members can be used to enrich the learning of all. The church as a body with mutually dependent members exemplifies this process.

Honey and Mumford in *Using your Learning Style* (copyright but available from Peter Honey) suggest the following activities and experiences suit the different learning styles:

The Activist Learning Style

A person with a preference for the activist style will learn best from activities and experiences in which:

— there are new experiences, problems, or opportunities to learn from.

— they get closely involved in participating activities, especially such things as business games, competitive teamwork tasks, role playing exercises, etc.

— there is excitement, drama, or crisis, and a good deal of variety with a range of diverse activities which they are required to tackle.

— they get a good deal of attention focused on their own role in the learning situation — perhaps as chairperson of the group, leader of the discussion, presenter of the data.

— there is freedom to generate ideas without them being shaped by "external" constraints like policy guidelines, predetermined structures, or the need to consider questions like practicability.

— they get thrown in at the deep end with a task that seems difficult to accomplish because of seemingly inadequate resources or adverse conditions.

— the learning involves working with other people in a team to bounce ideas about and solve problems jointly.

Activist learners will not learn so well, and may react against learning situations where:

— learning involves a passive role, as in listening to lectures, sermons, explanations, or papers being read, or in watching without being able to participate.

— they are asked to stand back and not be involved.

— they are expected to assimilate, analyse and interpret lots of detailed data.

— they have to work on their own (e.g. reading, writing, thinking).

— they are asked to assess beforehand what they hope to learn, and to evaluate what they have learned afterwards.

— they are expected to master "theoretical" statements like explanations of causality or background.

— they are expected to perform one activity over and over again (e.g. when practising a manipulative skill).

— the instructions they have to follow leave little freedom for individual action.

— they are expected to give closer attention to minor details.

The Theorist Learning Style

By contrast, someone with a preference for theorism as a learning style will learn best from activities in which:

— the theoretical basis is clear and the relationship of the activity to the overall system, concept or model is given a high profile.

— there is time for methodical exploration of the associations and relationships between ideas, events and situations.

— there is an opportunity to prove the methodology, assumptions or logic behind the activity, to test it for coherence.

— they are intellectually stretched (e.g. by having to engage in complex analysis, or answer searching questions posed by people with sharp, analytical minds).

— there is a clear structure and purpose.

— the ideas and concepts on offer emphasize logic and rationality, and are elegantly presented and supported by watertight arguments.

— they can analyse and then generalize the reasons for failure and success.

— there are interesting ideas on offer, even though these may not be immediately relevant.

— participation in and understanding of complex situations is required.

The theorist, however, will have difficulty in situations where:

— the context or purpose of the activity is unclear, especially if she/he is thrown in at the deep end.

— there is an emphasis on emotions and feelings.

— activities are unstructured, and there is a high degree of ambiguity, uncertainty or open-endedness.

— decisions must be taken without a conceptual basis being established.

— doubt exists at to the methodological soundness of date (e.g. arguments advanced without supporting statistics).

— there is little opportunity for in-depth exploration of the subject.

— there is a high proportion of non-theorist participants, especially activists.

The Reflector Learning Style

People who prefer to learn by reflection will be most at ease in situations where:

— they are encouraged to watch, think, or chew over what is going on.

— they can stand back from events and observe them (e.g. observing a fishbowl exercise, watching a film or audio visual presentation).

— they are allowed to think before acting, and have time to prepare and assimilate before commenting.

— painstaking research is possible.

— there is an opportunity to review what has happened and what has been learned.

— they are asked to produce carefully considered analytical responses to the activity.

— exchange of views takes place with a well-structured situation which minimizes risk of personal disagreement and confrontation.

— there is time to reach a decision without deadlines.

Reflectors will be least likely to learn well where:

— they are forced into the limelight, especially if this involves taking risks (e.g. in role play).

— they are expected to engage in action without planning.

— they are asked without warning for instant reactions or off-the-cuff ideas.

— there is insufficient data on which to base a conclusion.

— they are given inflexible instructions about how things should be done.

— they are under pressure of time.

— it becomes necessary for reasons of expediency to make short cuts.

The Pragmatist Learning Style

A person who prefers the pragmatist learning style will learn most effectively when:

— there is no obvious link between the subject matter and some practical aspect of the job.

— the learning emphasizes advantageous techniques of performance (e.g. ways to save time, deal with difficult people, etc.).

— there is a credible expert who can offer coaching as they try out and practise techniques.

— they are presented a with model for emulation (e.g. a film of how it is done, a respected individual to emulate).

— they are given techniques whose relevance to their own jobs is clear.

— there is immediate opportunity to practise what has been learned.

— the learning activity is one in which they feel they are grappling with "real" problems.

— it is possible to concentrate on practical issues like action plans with an obvious end product.

Pragmatist learners, however, will learn least in situations where:

— they cannot see any immediate relevance in what they are learning.

— the teacher or the situation seems remote from reality, "ivory-towered".

— there is no opportunity to practise anything, or no clear guidelines on how to do it.

— the learning appears to be going round in circles.

— there are political, structural or personal obstacles to implementing what has been learned.

— the learning activity seems to have no adequate reward.

Used by kind permission of
Peter Honey and Alan
Mumford and the Lichfield
Diocese.